Martha Marek And Other Female Serial Killers

Pete Dove

Published by Trellis Publishing, 2021.

While every precaution has been taken in the preparation of this book, the publisher assumes no responsibility for errors or omissions, or for damages resulting from the use of the information contained herein.

MARTHA MAREK AND OTHER FEMALE SERIAL KILLERS

First edition. July 4, 2021.

Copyright © 2021 Pete Dove.

ISBN: 979-8224692187

Written by Pete Dove.

MARSHA MAREK & OTHER FEMALE SERIAL KILLERS

PETE DOVE

Marsh Marek – The Viennese Poisoner

Vienna is one of the world's most beautiful cities. Its architecture is without precedent. Whether taking in the breath-taking views from the giddying heights of St Stephen's Cathedral, or admiring the turrets and towers of the City Hall, Vienna is a feast for the eyes.

And the stomach. Little on Earth beats sitting at a street side table in some Viennese café, rich coffee in front and the velvet taste of sumptuous Sache Torte scintillating the taste buds. It seems almost sacrilegious to remind ourselves that some of Austria's past leaves the bitter taste of dubious morality.

The nation – or its leaders at least – had put up little resistance to Hitler's annexation of the country in early 1938. In fact, the rampant Nazi party in the landlocked country had welcomed the Fascist regime with open arms.

Indeed, Hitler was so confident of a cheery welcome that he accompanied his troops as they marched into Austria, and received the kind of greeting normally reserved for heroes rather than conquering leaders. Not every citizen was pleased to see the neighbours march through the door, however. Particularly so the Jewish community in Austria, along with those from the Romany population, patients who suffered from mental illness and the hidden homosexual inhabitants.

Martha Marek was another who would soon be looking on the invaders with a jaundiced eye. As somebody considered half Jewish, she would already have plenty to worry about. But, as we will see, Adolf Hitler was about to play a significant role in her ultimate and, many would argue, deserved demise.

Martha was born into almost as unpleasant circumstances as those in which she would later die. She was born and very quickly abandoned. Unsurprisingly, under these circumstances, there is a lot of uncertainty around her early years. Even the year and place of her birth are reported variously. Some accounts list her birth date and place as 1904 in Vienna; others report her as entering the world at the turn of the century. Still more identify her place of birth as Sopron, which is in Hungary. The safest conclusion is that she was born somewhere in central Europe during the early years of the twentieth century,

What happened next is equally unclear. The most probable explanation of her earliest years is that she spent a few months with her mother – her biological father is unknown – before being fostered by a kindly couple, a chef and his wife.

However, while still a toddler, her real mother married Rudolph Lowenstein, who was the station master in the town of Baden, close to the Austrian capital. Young Martha was then able to re-join her mother. However, playing happy families was just not to be for the Lowenstein clan. By the time Martha was seven, the station master had bought a one way ticket to America – alone. Once more, Martha's mother felt that she could not cope with a small child, and the girl found herself this time living in a charity home in Vienna.

She re-joined her mother again at twelve, and earned some pennies running errands for a dress shop. Then, when she was around the age of thirteen, Martha's life took a significant and twisted turn.

Once again, exact details are sketchy – many of them based on Martha's own, somewhat selective, memories. Morlitz Fritsch was a wealthy department store owner whose expensive shop occupied a place in the heart of Vienna's downtown. The time in question was, according to Martha, set in the years leading up to the World War. Fritsch was already sixty two when he first set eyes on the child, waif like and hungry looking, as she travelled on a streetcar.

He was immediately fascinated by the young girl; he engaged her in conversation and indicated that as she had experience working in a dress shop, he might be able to find her better paid employment in his own store. It takes little reading between the lines to at least suspect that Fritsch's intentions were not exactly noble.

He contacted the young girl's mother and very soon she was ensconced in his luxurious villa in the wealthy Moedling district of

Vienna. Martha became officially listed as his ward. Depending on her actual age when she entered his home, the claims of what happened next fit somewhere between the rather uncomfortable and the downright illegal. It is alleged that Fritsch saw in his young ward more than the chance to do good and offer the down at heel girl (and, later, her half sister whom he also adopted) the best education money could buy. Instead, his interest was, at least in part, sexual. Or so some investigators into Martha Marek's life are keen to claim. Other, kinder, commentators describe the magnate as 'hearty' and 'generous'.

Whichever is the truer take, certainly, his own son and daughter were sufficiently unimpressed by the new arrangements that they moved out of the house, and went instead to live with their mother, whom Fritsch had divorced in 1900.

Although getting on in years, Fritsch was a healthy and energetic man, and his death at the age of 74 was something a surprise. A suspicious one. Rumours were bandied about that the wealthy department store owner had been helped on his way with poison.

The allegation was hard to prove. Neither his son or daughter were keen to have their father's body exhumed and examined. Scandal would certainly follow such a move and that would be harmful for business. In any case, although their inheritance was less than it might have been, they still became very wealthy young people when their father's will was enacted.

So, too, did his young ward. From penniless urchin, by the time she was in her early twenties Martha was a rich girl in her own right. She intended to enjoy her new-found status. Within three months of her lover's death, Martha was married. Her husband was a student, Emil Marek, who was studying at the Vienna Technical Institute. Unusually for the time, Emil married an older woman – just - Martha being just three years his senior.

The extent to which he was in love is uncertain. He could have just been bowled over by the attentions of a woman who would have seemed a wealthy sophisticate in his eyes. More certain is that Emil was not the strongest character. He was so embarrassed at having a wife older than he that he immediately left his studies, and grew a wispy beard in the hope that it might make him seem more mature.

While at his college, Emil's subject had been engineering. With money behind him, albeit his wife's, he set about launching unworkable scheme after unlikely engineering project. One of these was the electrification of Burgenland, which was Austria's least technically advanced province. Astonishingly, the inexperienced, young and failed student persuaded the Government to match the money he was prepared to put into the project. Sensing that he and Martha were about to turn from the category of very comfortably off to the exclusive club of the super rich, he took the forward thinking step of insuring his life. No doubt, under the encouragement of his wife.

It was a decision he would come to regret.

He took out the insurance with the Anglo-Danubian Lloyd Company, which was based in Vienna. In the even of his death, his wife would receive a hearty sum equivalent in today's money of $100000. Even more impressively, permanent disability would earn him four times that amount. His first premium was made on June 11th 1925.

Clearly, the decision to start the policy from that date was fortuitous. Very, very fortuitous. Because on the exact next day, June 12th 1925, the following unfortunate incident occurred: Emil was working at home, in the garden of the Moedling Villa he shared with Martha. He was chopping a block of wood when the razor sharp tool slipped. A scream burst from his lips, one no doubt muffled by his bravery, but sufficient to attract Martha and Paula, her half-sister. They emerged to see Emil lying prostrate, blood pouring from his leg. This, in turn, was dangling almost in two, the halves connected by no more than a sinew. Stoically, Martha called the doctor who, seeing that the leg was impossible to save, promptly cut it off.

We know that this is the order of events because it is what Martha and Emil told the insurance company, their story so neatly put together it must have been true. Surely. Who could doubt it? For the insurers Emil's accident was about to prove costly. A nasty accident led to permanent disability. $400000 please.

Unsurprisingly, the Anglo-Danubian Insurance Company was more than a tad suspicious. They travelled to the Moedling hospital and examined the leg. It appeared as though Emil was even braver than suspected. Remarkably, it appeared, he had continued with his chopping even after the first blow fell into his lower limb. In fact, the same thing had happened twice more. The leg showed evidence of three separate blows.

But then the intrigue deepened. Karl Mraz had been an orderly at the hospital, and he would be happy to tell any trial that there was more to the savaged leg than met the eye. That was because, he would testify, he had overheard doctors discussing that the insurance company was paying them to 'fix' the leg so it appeared as though it had been struck three times. That Mraz was being paid by the Mareks to give this testimony was conveniently omitted from his evidence. Further, the fact that Mraz was also observed entering and leaving the Marek's villa was, of course, purely coincidental...if rather inconvenient to the defense.

The couple were arrested, but when the matter came to court it found in their favour. Partly. The court decided the couple were not guilty of defrauding their insurers, but they did receive a small sentence each for their involvement with Mraz's lies. However, they had already been held in custody and much to public joy – the couple were front page news and generally seen as young heroes against the wicked insurance company – were immediately released. In the end, the insurance company settled for about the equivalent of $50000 in Austrian marks, much of which was used by the Marek's to pay their legal costs.

But if luck was with them at that time, it soon went away. Or, perhaps more accurately, the couple's atrocious business plans contributed to their change in fortune. Fritsch's money was long gone, wasted on good living and bad ideas, and the insurance monies quickly followed. Among the more ludicrous plans of the impractical young couple were a taxi fleet that quickly drove itself out of business; a plan to build utilities in North Africa that sent their monies rapidly down the drain and a planned vegetable market that harvested nothing.

During these tough times family life deteriorated. Martha began to hate her failure of a husband, a man whose ideas were only matched in their frailty by his health. The couple did manage two children in that time, Alfons was born in 1929 and Ingeborg came along three years later. But their money was gone, and they sold the villa to pay off debts and moved to a far less salubrious part of the city.

In fact, money was so tight that Emil returned part time to his parents, taking meals with them and, remarkably, gaining health. It was only when he returned to his wife that illness returned. This time, with a vengeance. Within a month, his eyesight had failed and the invalid lost weight with astonishing rapidity. He was admitted to hospital, where he died on July 31st 1932. His death certificate listed tuberculosis as the cause of his passing.

Martha really did seem feted to the most unfortunate, luckless spell. Or her family did. Within a few weeks of her husband's death, young Ingeborg became ill. As if often the case with a small child, the cause of her sickness was very difficult for doctors to pinpoint. All that they knew was she went downhill fast, and tragically on September 2nd of the same year her father died, so did she. Just one month and two days passed between the deaths of Martha's husband and her daughter.

Fortunately for the grieving woman, the pain of her husband's and daughter's terrible deaths were eased a little. Both had been insured, and each bereavement earned her a pay-out. At least the young woman could stop peddling vegetables on the streets. At least she could spend more time being a caring mother to her remaining child.

Astonishingly, or not as it turns out, Alfons was the next to fall ill. It seemed as though some terrible canker was attacking the family one by one. Of course, that was true, although the it was a disease from within the home that was causing all of the danger and destruction. Still the authorities suspected nothing. Perhaps the root of their failure to act lay in Martha herself. She was young, attractive and even though she might not be the socialite she once was, there was a residue of glamour attached to her. Relatively recently she had been the public's pin up girl, the woman who successfully took on that most hated of institutions, an insurance company. It was inconceivable that the misfortune striking her family down was the result of her own actions.

This time, there was some good news. Alfons' illness was caught quickly enough by doctors. Probably more by chance than good medicine, whatever treatments they offered him worked. His decline was halted and the young boy steadily recovered from the mysterious ailment that had afflicted him. Of course, with hindsight it is quite reasonably to draw the conclusion that Alfons' life was saved simply because he was hospitalized and was therefore away from his mother. Healthy, unadulterated food allied to the good fortune of having been hospitalized before irreparable damage had been done were the reasons that he survived.

Matters settled down. For eighteen months nothing untoward attacked the Marek family. Martha began to look further afield for the chance to find some funds, and discovered that a distant Aunt – elderly, mostly neglected and, crucially, reasonably well off – had turned into a lonely old woman. Suzanne Lowenstein was sixty seven, and her marriage to a member of the Lowenstein brood brought her under Martha's radar. That uncle had been an army surgeon but had died, leaving his wife with a tidy sum.

Martha began to take an interest in the elderly Aunt. She was a skilled manipulator of people, as able to charm an elderly woman as easily as she could lure a man into her bedroom. Aunt Suzanne was delighted by the interest shown by her debonair young niece, a lady who appeared to have herself fallen so unfortunately on hard times.

Indeed, it made total sense for the poor unfortunate to move into her rambling home, and act as a friendly, live in, companion to her. In fact, she was so flattered by the attentions she received that she decided it was time to re-write her will. The elderly lady instructed her lawyer to make Martha Marek, caring niece and victim of life's unpredictable slings and arrows, her main beneficiary. In fact, her sole beneficiary.

That was in the summer of 1934. In June she had begun to show symptoms of some kind of vague illness. In the beginning of July the will was changed, and Aunt Suzanne started to go properly downhill. Her sight deteriorated rapidly. Her mobility faltered, and soon she was bed-ridden. Her hair began to fall out by the handful, and her eyesight failed. Her decline from slightly dotty, but active, Aunt to invalid was astonishingly fast. Whatever illness had afflicted her, doctors concluded, must be virulent indeed. So virulent, in fact, that on July 17th she died.

Still, the blow to Martha was eased a little. She had the inheritance her Aunt had left. She could remain in the comfortably rented apartment her Aunt had lived in, and enjoy the expensive furnishings willed to her. And thanks to her usual resilience in the face of tragedy, her period of mourning was short. Very quickly, Martha was spending lavishly once more. Her aunt's money would not last her for long.

Jeno Neumann was an insurance salesman who had the misfortune to become acquainted with Martha. Although, at forty nine, he was a good deal older than the would be socialite, as with most men she was able to both manipulate him, and dominate him. He moved into the luxurious home and became a sub tenant, and then the latest in a long line of lovers Martha enjoyed.

Being involved in insurance was a handy attribute as far as Martha was concerned. Cynics might even suggest that this experience made Neumann a more attractive proposition than any good looks or witty mind he might possess. (These is no evidence that the poor man benefitted from either of these characteristics.)

Martha decided to let another room in the house, and advertised for a tenant. After an appropriate period of due diligence with regards to applicants, she settled on a fifty three year old seamstress, Felicitas Kittenberger, to become her lodger. At the same time as offering a room, she was also able to reassure Mrs Kittenberger that, thanks to her many wealthy friends and associates, there would be plenty of work heading her way.

The next stage of her scheme was to persuade Neumann to issue an insurance policy for Mrs Kittenberger; and, as landlord Martha Marek was named as the bearer in the event that the tenant should have the misfortune to become deceased. Remarkably, she quickly became ill. The poor tenant lost the use of her legs; her eyes began to fail and each morning her pillow would be littered with locks of hair. On June 2nd 1934 the unfortunate seamstress died. Once more, the shock for Martha was alleviated by an insurance pay-out of, after taxes, the equivalent (in contemporary money) of just under $800.

But if Martha was not overly distressed by the outcome, the same could not be said for Mrs Kittenberger's son, Herbert. He confronted his mother's landlady, and accused her of murder. With remarkable composure, Martha simply called the police and had him arrested, although in the circumstances he was let off with a warning and sent on his way.

Events in the Marek household went remarkably quiet for a couple of years. Then, in October 1936, Martha attempted a different money raising scheme. In some ways, it was the least harmful of all her methods of getting cash. It did not involve her hacking off her husband's leg with an axe. Nobody was killed. But it did lead to her downfall.

Inspector of the Vienna police Rudolph Peternell had no idea that he was about to become involved in one of the most infamous crimes in Austrian history (Nazism aside). On October 31st 1936 he headed out to a comfortable part of the city in order to speak to the victim of a burglary. The woman he saw at the somewhat overbearing apartment made an immediate impression. Flame haired and attractive in a manicured, sophisticated way, she was also suffering from some obvious recent illness. She limped around the apartment, using her hands to feel her way. One hand, in fact, because the other hung limply by her side.

The reason for her struggles were, the lady told the inspector, that she was recovering from a recent stroke. Both her sight and her mobility had been affected.

Peternell set to work with a standard array of questions. Mrs Marek had, she told the officer, sent her maid home early the previous night as the young girl wished to see a movie. Then, she had retired to bed at her usual time with nothing amiss. The next day, however, Mrs Marek had realised there was something very wrong indeed.

'In the morning,' she said, her voice frail sounding, 'on entering the drawing room, I soon discovered that certain articles were missing. Not only tapestries and paintings, but jewellery.'

Peternell asked whether there had been aware of anything unusual during the night. Her answer seemed, on the face of it, plausible.

'Ever since suffering a stroke,' she explained as a reason for hearing nothing of the burglary, 'I have been a very heavy sleeper.'

The conversation moved on until it reached the tricky question of the extent of the robbery. Martha Marek told the officer that property worth about two and a half thousand dollars (or the equivalent in Austrian marks) had been lost. On questioning, she confirmed that she had insurance which covered almost the entire amount.

Peternell made a list of the missing articles, and headed back to the station. It was while he was travelling to his headquarters that a couple of questions sprung to his mind. Even by the end of 1936, Martha Marek enjoyed a kind of limited local notoriety – everyone loves a poor girl made good. He recalled reading recently that she had been seen at a party in a local dance hall. He recalled no mention made of any ill health, and thought it odd that a woman so apparently disabled should attend such a party, and even odder that, having done so, reporters had not picked up on the human interest story of her physical decline. Strange.

Then he thought back to the itinerary he had made of missing items. Tapestries are large, heavy and easily identified. In fact, exactly the sort of thing a thief would avoid unless stealing to order. On the other hand, the apartment had been littered with valuable looking pieces of silver – items easily transportable and simple to sell on. Peternell reported his doubts to his superiors. They listened, and decided to look into Martha Marek's file...if she had one. They soon realised that she did indeed have a dossier of past incidents. An extremely bulky one. Martha Marek was, they decided, a woman worth keeping a close eye on.

Peternell and a colleague, Josef Gunacker, were charged with maintaining a watch on their subject. And with making enquiries.

One of the most remarkable things about Martha Marek was that she got away with things for so long. It is amazing what a careful back story, good looks and a bit of luck can achieve, because what was for certain was that she was not a great criminal.

The detectives spoke to the janitor of the block where she lived, and he reported seeing her moving a number of large bundles to a truck on the evening of October 31st, the night her robbery was supposed to have occurred. To the janitor, she seemed in her normal state of good health. The notion that she was suffering the after-effects of a stroke were an embroidery of her story which was neither thought through, nor sustainable.

The detectives hunted out the storage warehouse where Martha's bundles had been delivered on the night of October 31st. They were, unsurprisingly, the very ones she had reported as being stolen.

Next Peternell persuaded Martha's cleaning lady to lie to her mistress. In return for a handy sum, she told Martha that, on a particular day, she would be unable to attend but would send a substitute cleaner instead. The lady who turned up worked for the police, and soon confirmed that Martha was as healthy as she.

Clear in their minds that Martha's report of having been burgled was no more than a fraudulent attempt to get some insurance money, they turned their attentions to the more serious matters of the oddly high number of people who met a premature end after they became close to Martha Marek. The bodies of her husband Emil, her daughter Ingeborg, he aunt and lodger were exhumed. An investigation, even one as primitive as those that were used pre-war,' indicated a large quantity of the chemical thallium present in the corpses. This is often used as a rat poison. Investigations suggested that Martha Marek must have a long standing problem with rats, wherever she was living, because she was a regular purchaser of the product.

She was arrested, and her trial began on May 2nd 1938. It was to be a spectacular affair. In Austria at the time capital punishment was available to the courts and employed the especially gruesome method of beheading by guillotine. Confessing to her crimes would undoubtedly have led to the 'Devil in Petticoats', as she was dubbed in the popular press, escaping such a fate. But, despite the many efforts of the prosecutor to inveigle a confession from her, Martha would do no such thing. Indeed, such was the venom with which she stared at the attorney that on one occasion he told her: 'Don't try to hypnotize me madam!'

Indeed, Martha seemed determined to turn the whole trial into a fiasco. At one point she told the prosecutor: 'I wish you would be as good a father as I am a mother.' Even the judge did not escape her ire. 'You know more about stealing than I do,' she told him after he asked about a theft.

But her protests were in vain. The prosecution had over fourteen hundred pages of evidence and a hundred witnesses. Crucial among them were the detectives variously hired by insurance companies she had defrauded. Another, a pharmacist, reported selling her so much rat poison that he had had to increase his wholesale supply.

Still, when the inevitable verdict of guilt was cast, and Martha was sentenced to death, nobody thought it would happen. No woman had been executed in Austria for thirty years, none in Vienna for sixty. But they had not counted on Hitler becoming involved. He had his own executioner in his employ, and was determined that a hard line must be followed.

Johann Reichart killed more than 3000 people in his role as Hitler's leading criminal executioner. Martha Marek would prove to be one of the more challenging of his career. As she awaited her fate, once more she claimed to have lost use of her legs, but Reichart was a professional. His team practised tipping a wheelchair until its occupant fell straight onto the guillotine block.

As she was wheeled from her cell, by some kind of miracle Martha regained her mobility and fought fiercely against the violent fate awaiting her. She even managed to hit the cold eyed superstar executioner with a sharp kick. But she was overpowered, thrown onto the guillotine and, struggling until the last, despatched with one sharp fall of the blade.

There is a more than a touch of the macabre about the case of Martha Marek, even down to her alliterative name. She could easily feature in a late night Hallowe'en drama, one aiming to raise as many laughs as screams. Her inability to chop off her husband's leg in one blow, her pathetic attempts to appear disabled from a stroke, even her bizarre outbursts at her trial, all seem more at home in the pages of second rate fiction than the records of a capital court.

But we should not forget that she was a callous killer, one who murdered people she knew for personal greed. Included in her catalogue of victims, of course, are not only her husband but her baby daughter as well. As far as we know, only one of her intended victims survived: her son, Alfons. At Martha's trial a witness, neighbour Eugenie Hellinger, put the evil of Martha Marek into perspective. She told the court that Alfons had said the following to her, one day, before being rescued from his own poisoning.

'I shall soon go to Heaven,' he told the neighbor. 'My mother told me so.'

WHEN GIRLS NEXT DOOR KILL : THE TRUE STORY OF CINDY COLLIER & SHIRLEY WOLF
IRIS OWEN

"Today, Cindy and I ran away and killed an old lady. It was lots of fun" -
Shirley Wolf's journal, June 14th, 1983.

Shirley Wolf and Cindy Collier met in a juvenile detention center and had known each other for only a few hours when they decided to escape and randomly kill a stranger.

They would go to a senior condominium center in Auburn, California where they would seek an elderly victim.

They would find one in the eighty-five-year-old Anna Brackett. They entered her home under the ruse that they needed to use the phone to call their parents.

The girls would brutally murder the elderly woman in a crime so shocking that deputy sheriffs were initially in denial that two young girls would commit such a crime.

But how did they get to the point mentally where they could commit such a horrid act? This is the story of how they got there.

EARLY LIFE

Cindy Collier wasn't the nice girl next door. Her entire body language spoke of rage and hostility. By the age of twelve, she was a regular at the juvenile hall where she would routinely assaulting staff and inmate alike.

Incorrigible, she had been arrested for burglary, theft and drug possession.

Because of her age, Cindy was often spared jail time and was sentenced to community service. She would most often be sent to pick up litter on highways but the punishment wasn't enough to deter her from a life of crime.

"She was a smart ass towards everyone," former classmate Mike Fluty said.

No one was spared her rage. At fourteen years old, she had no problem harassing adults as well, randomly accosting people on the street.

"What are you looking at?" she asked a woman walking by as she smoked a cigarette. "You think you're better than me?"

She would then raise her fist to the woman and force her to run away. "Oooh!" Cindy taunted. "Ooooh! Come on, you want some?"

"Cindy liked to intimidate," forensic psychologist Paula Orange said. "She had learned it was better to be a predator than the prey very early on in life. Her early childhood would shape the monster she would become."

Cindy's parents divorced when she was one year old. Her mother would remarry but that would end in divorce as well. She would take care of Cindy and her three sons during the day and go to a waitress job at night.

Cindy stated that she had been raped by an undisclosed family member and by another man who threw her down a flight of stairs after he finished with her.

"Her mother reportedly had different children all by different men," Orange said. "Cindy was molested by one of her mother's endless string of men that she brought into the home."

Cindy would talk about her "rotten" childhood and describe being "raped a few times." She tried to commit suicide on several occasions but that only brought her more frustrations. So instead of harming herself, she decided she would harm others.

"I want them to pay," she said.

By the time she entered Chana High in Auburn, California, Cindy had a well-established reputation of someone who should be feared. Using physical intimidation, she would randomly choose a girl she didn't like and the bullying would begin. She would push and yell, getting in their face. Her victims would be spared no quarter, on one occasion, Cindy ripped the blouse of a girl and forced her to run down the street topless.

"She was a trained bully," Orange said. "She knew exactly how to push the buttons of her victims, strip them of their dignity. It was done to her at home so it was easy for her to pass along the abuse."

Cindy was a menacing presence on campus to the other petite girls. At 5'9" and 140 pounds, she could beat up any girl in the school. She had a strong jawline and broad shoulders but it was her eyes that set her apart from the average bully. Eyes that pierced through her victims and gave them an implicit message.

I want to kill you.

Cindy's crimes would not be limited to physical assaults. She would grab and take whatever she wanted. She would go into liquor stores, stuff food into her pockets and leave. She would go into malls and steal cassette tapes at the record store. After a few months, she graduated to stealing a car. This would land her in a juvenile detention center where she would be a kindred spirit unlike any other she had met before.

LIKE LOOKING INTO A MIRROR

Like Cindy, Shirley Wolf had been the victim of sexual abuse. Her father, Louis Wolf, would rape her. But the abuse didn't stop with just her father. She was a molested by her paternal grandfather and uncle as well.

An observant kindergarten teacher noticed the odd behavior of Shirley and recommended that she get psychiatric help to no avail.

Shirley didn't know where else to turn as she would be abused by all of the men in her life. At the age of six years old, she had run away for the first time. The streets were too rough for her, however, and she was scared back home by the dark characters of Brooklyn.

A lost little girl with nowhere else to go but the house where she was abused.

Her father, Louis, worked as a carpenter but suffered an accident that forced him to take disability. He would remain at home and begin bossing his children around. Then it turned to the sexual abuse of his daughter, Shirley.

When Shirley was around six, the family would move from the east coast to Placerville, California so Louis could be closer to his own family.

Louis Wolf would send Shirley's mother Katherine on an errand to get some groceries one morning. He then locked Shirley's three younger brothers out of the house and turned his attention to Shirley.

He cornered her in the bathroom and raped her.

Shirley would never forgive her father for what he did to her.

Louis would rape his daughter sometimes as much as three times per day. By the time she reached puberty, he put her on birth control.

Shirley never told her mother because she didn't want to break up the family.

Louis would tell Shirley to not tell her mother what he had done. Shirley obliged only because she was afraid how badly the news would hurt her mother.

Eventually, however, the abuse became so intolerable that she told her mother.

Her mother suspected it all along. She then went to the authorities.

Louis would deny that he molested Shirley but plead guilty to reduced charges which brought his sentencing down to a mere one-hundred days.

Louis was told that if he fought the charges, he would be facing fifty years. So he took the three months.

Shirley would then be removed from the home which was her worst fear. She would be bounced from foster home to foster home where she told of feeling "like a stranger."

"You get to the point where you're pushed in a corner and I just came back fighting," Shirley said. "I want to go home. I forgive my father and I try to forget it. He's apologized to me, my family and to God."

A MATCH TO A FLAME

It would be only fitting that the first time the girls would meet, it would be under the guise of violence.

At the detention center, Shirley was being beaten to a pulp by a fellow inmate in the hallway. As per usual, no guards were around. But Cindy stood her ground against the bigger girl, to no avail.

The girl threw her against the wall, punched her in the stomach and twisted her arm.

"Who are you?" Cindy asked as she came upon the two girls fighting.

"Shirley Wolf."

"I like you, Shirley Wolf."

And with that, Cindy got her opponent into a full nelson, easily overpowering Shirley's tormentor.

"Let her have it," Cindy said.

Shirley didn't hesitate. She began pummeling the girl, all of the rage of being abused all of her life came forth as she gave the girl a beat-down.

Cindy threw the girl to the ground and the two laughed as she moaned in pain.

"Later loser," Shirley sniffed.

Cindy laughed. The girl had spunk and they spent the next couple of hours exchanging their life stories.

For some reason, Cindy did not feel hatred toward Shirley. She felt like they had an unspoken bond but she didn't know why.

The truth was, they were both ticking time bombs.

"I think it was an unfortunate chemistry between the two girls," Shirley's defense attorney Thomas Condit said. "I think it also had to do with finding a new friend and wanting to show that she was capable of doing anything that the friend was."

Shirley was the opposite of Cindy in one regard, however, as she did not have Cindy's assurance. Shirley felt "hopeless and helpless" as she talked about running away from the detention center. She talked about this as if it were an impossibility, a faraway dream.

But Cindy felt otherwise. She behaved as if she knew all the answers.

"I can get us out of here," Cindy said with total assurance.

"You can?"

"Sure. I do it all the time. But we're going to need a car. This place where I used to live as all kinds of old people. We can steal one of their cars. But we'll probably have to kill them."

"Yeah," Shirley said.

"You know," Cindy said. "In case one of them rats us out."

Cindy led the way as the girls escaped. They talked about how they would put their sadistic plan in motion. They wanted to find someone old and feeble...someone who could not fight back...someone who they could kill for fun.

"I suppose a good analogy would be to compare the girls to the boys from Columbine who would come over a decade later," Orange said. "One needed the other to pull off such a horrid act. They needed that voice over their shoulder to egg them on. They both wanted the same thing and together they could make it happen."

Both Cindy and Shirley would dye their hair red in order to disguise themselves. They then went "victim hunting," touring Cindy's old neighborhood in Auburn Green, a condo for senior citizens. They wanted a car. A nice one. So they began searching the parking lot for a car and would match the number on the parking slot to the condo number.

Then they would knock on the door. Their questions were innocent. They would ask for directions, a glass of water or ask to use the phone. But there was something about their demeanor, a sinister or insincere look in their eye that set off the alarm bells for all of the senior citizens they met. They were allowed inside by Joe Becker and his wife who gave them a glass of water. When they left, however, the elderly couple immediately washed the glass and scrubbed the phone with alcohol, the girls seemed so dirty.

"They were looking for an easy target," Orange said. "Becker was seventy but still probably too much of a hassle for them. They needed easy."

Then they knocked on the door of Anna Brackett.

"We decided we were going to kill her when we saw her," Shirley said. "She was just an old lady. Just a perfect setup. We killed her because we wanted her car and we didn't want to get caught."

Anna was a retired seamstress who worked for Sears. She had great-grandchildren who were the ages of Cindy and Shirley.

She was a helpful and kind person to all her knew her. She didn't hesitate in helping some girls that were the ages of her great-grandchildren.

"Can I help you?" Anna opened the door with a smile.

"Hi," Cindy said. "Can you please help us? We need to call our parents and the phone down the street is not working."

"Sure," Anna said, opening up her door.

Ann was congenial and didn't see any reason not to trust the girls. She let them into her home and the threesome chatted for over an hour. They sat on the couch and she gave them soda. She would show the girls pictures of her family. Pictures of her children, grandchildren.

"It is unusual for a sociopath to want to know about their victim," Orange said. "They really don't want to know their victim because it humanizes them. So perhaps the teen girls were hesitant at first. But it was more of a case of them working up the nerve to do what they set out to do."

The phone rang and Anna went up to answer it.

The call came from her son.

"I'm on my way," her son said.

"Okay," Anna said, hanging up the phone. "I'm sorry, girls. My son is coming to pick me up. We're going to the bingo parlor."

"Now," Cindy said as the girls pounced.

Shirley grabbed the elderly woman by the throat and slammed her to the ground.

"What are you doing?" Anna screamed. "What are you doing?"

Cindy sprinted to the kitchen and rifled through the drawers. She found a butcher knife and gave it to Shirley.

"Do it," Cindy commanded.

Shirley would then stab the helpless old woman without mercy. She would recall stabbing her in the neck and "freaking out" because the old lady kept screaming.

"You're killing me!" Anna shouted.

"Good," Shirley said, slicing the knife down again. She would stop only when she saw the blood coming out of Anna's mouth.

Anna Brackett would suffer over twenty-eight stab wounds although the coroner believed it could have been more as the blade went through the same entry point. There was one stab wound where the blade had gone in four inches deep past Anna's breastplate.

"She died a horrific death," Orange said. "Painful and horrific. I've read some psychiatrists say that Shirley was getting revenge on all of the people that hurt her in the past, that in some way Anna symbolized her mother and she was killing her mother symbolically. I believe that is psychobabble. Shirley was not that bright. She was following the lead of Cindy and they wanted to kill and maim. That was the point. Not to subconsciously work out her anger. She was a defective unit."

Cindy then sifted through all of Anna's drawers and closets looking for money. They found the keys to the old woman's 1970 Dodge and ripped the two telephones from the wall.

They went into the garage and found out that the keys they had stolen would not start the car. Angered, they left the condo on foot and began hitch-hiking.

Ironically, Anna's son Carl would drive pass them on the street, ignoring the girls who had their thumbs out.

He then entered his mother's home and discovered her mutilated body on the floor.

It was a surreal scene for her son. His mother on the floor in a pool of blood. Trapped in his own real life horror movie, Carl would never have guessed that two underage girls would be capable of such a thing.

LIKE A DAY AT THE OFFICE

Cindy and Shirley made it to her home in Auburn. They turned on the television, eagerly awaiting news of the murder they had committed.

Too many people had spotted them around the neighborhood. In all, eleven people informed the investigating officers of the two red-headed girls with the strange demeanor.

Some remembered Cindy from when she lived with her grandparents in the condo development. The deputies, however, didn't believe that two teenage girls could have done what they did to Anna.

Back home, the girls would cheer as their murder was reported on the evening news.

Then they went to sleep.

At 2:30 a.m the deputies would arrive at the house of Cindy Collier.

Deputy George Coelho didn't believe the girls did the crime. But after a few minutes of questioning, Shirley confessed.

Cindy, however , would not only confess to the crime, she would gloat.

"She started to laugh," Deputy Coelho said.

Cindy expressed little remorse. She told the deputies that she felt like killing more people.

Shirley was excited and giddy as they had done something that "they had never done before."

They were placed under arrest and one of the deputies began reading her the Miranda rights. Shirley interrupted him, repeating the rights verbatim as she was already familiar with the process.

Cindy would tell the police that she felt jealousy toward anyone who appeared happy and normal. She felt such envy that she wanted to kill them.

The deputy expressed shock as Cindy detailed her desires of wanting to hurt people. She bragged about stabbing, shooting and throwing people into the Auburn Damn. The officers knew it was all bravado...with the exception of what they did to Ann Brackett.

The two girls would go to trial in July of 1983...a juvenile court.

What the girls wanted was fame and publicity.

They would get it as the brutal murder would be talked about in numerous high-profile magazines and the court case would reach a national audience. A movie called "Fun" was produced, chronicling the girl's first day together.

CRIME AND PUNISHMENT

Shirley's attorney, Thomas Condit, would enter a plea of not guilty by reason of insanity. "I'd like to say that Shirley felt sorry," Condit said. "But I can't. That's part of her problem. She told me that while she was killing the old lady, she was thinking of everybody she hated—her father and his mother. But the psychiatrist believes it was a symbolic killing of her own mother."

Both girls would receive the maximum imprisonment for underage girls. They would remain in jail until the age of twenty-five then be released.

"Shirley really can't understand the difference between right and wrong," Condit said. "How do you appreciate right and wrong when you have a father telling you it's wrong not to stay home and service him when you should be in school?"

THE AFTERMATH

Cindy would spend the next nine years at the California Youth Authority facility in Ventura. She would obtain an associate of arts degree then go on to study law at Pepperdine University. She would go on to have four children and live in Northern California without any further brushes with the law.

Shirley would be sent to the Central California Women's Facility near Chowchilla.

She would threaten other inmates and her jailers during her time in prison. She spent her days reading romance novels as she tries to take her mind off the tormented childhood which led her to be capable of such a crime.

"I think of my dad and it hurts," Shirley said. "I'll just feel pain and I'll have to cry to get it out. I can't really pinpoint where it's from. God knows, I'll get hurt and just cry."

Shirley would complete her high school education and become a born-again Christian. The attempts to improve her life would prove futile, however.

She had tried to contact her parents but they never returned her calls or letters. Finally, in the summer of 1992, Shirley tracked down the number of her parents in the Pacific Northwest. Louis, the man who had molested her, would answer her call.

They had not spoken in four years but he had told her that her mother had left him a few months prior, leaving the three young boys with him. Shirley asked about her favorite brother, L.J., but her father avoided giving her a straight answer.

Shirley wanted desperately to know what happened to her younger brother but could not locate him anywhere. Her father would then stop returning her calls.

On June 30th, 1995, Shirley would be freed from prison after serving twelve years for the murder of Anna Brackett.

Her father would die in 2002.

Unlike Cindy, Shirley's life of petty crimes would continue. She would get involved in prostitution, theft, and burglaries. She has shown remorse for the murder but also stated that "there is no going back."

Both women are now free, getting leniency for the crime because of their age. Their light sentences would draw the ire of Anna's son, Carl, who would rage at the judicial system that gave his mother no justice.

BETTY LOU WILL KILL YOU

29

ALICE WILSON

Betty Lou Beets is a perfect historical example of how multifaceted crime can be, how a victim could become an aggressor, or an aggressor may adopt the mask of victimhood, and how all is not necessarily as it seems. Convicted for murdering two men and assaulting or attempting to kill four, Betty Lou's story is one that would send chills down the spine of any man from any era. Only the fourth woman to be executed for murder, despite the overall statistics hovering around forty to fifty cases of capital punishment per year, her crimes were too gruesome and cold for the court to offer her a lesser sentence... or were they? As we shall see when we delve into her history, despite Betty Lou's extensive criminal record and constant charges against her from ex husbands and her own children, the justice system was eager to give her a way out of the death sentence and allow her to live her natural life out in prison. And although there were some mitigating circumstances, it is telling that Betty Lou Beets almost got away with a life sentence in a situation where many others would have been executed without remorse.

Betty Lou Beets was born Betty Lou Dunevant on the 12th of March 1937, in Roxboro, North Carolina, USA. Her parents were initially tobacco farmers, whose main pleasure in life was alcohol, resulting in rampant alcoholism and a violent family life not atypical of the rural poor of the Great Depression. They lived on a diet of salt pork and various flours, barely touching vegetables or fruit, let alone eggs, fish, nuts or pulses, essential for developing a healthy brain and body. Furthermore, Betty Lou was disabled. She was not completely deaf, but hard of hearing due to having contracted the measles some time between the ages of three and six. Her fever was so severe and prolonged that she suffered damage to her brain and ears. As her hearing was affected at such a young age, she suffered an impairment to her speech similar to what many deaf or hard of hearing children suffer. At another time, or in another family, Betty Lou may have received treatment and hearing aids, but as a poor family in 1940, they could not afford to get her the treatment she would have needed to hear and speak normally. Her education was strongly impacted as she could not learn to read or study, resulting in borderline illiteracy and innumeracy and a frustrating life at home and away. Betty Lou also claimed she had been raped by her father in early childhood, as well as sexually abused by others. By the age of twelve her family life was falling apart. Her mother had been institutionalized due to breakdowns caused by alcoholism and Betty Lou had to drop out of school so she could care for her younger brother and sister. Her father, who seemed to see her as a surrogate mother for her siblings, became guarded against any sign of Betty Lou escaping and would beat her for not taking full responsibility for her siblings. She was often at the doctor's office or in hospital for the injuries he inflicted on her. She finally left school completely. The family moved to Hampton, Virginia, while Betty Lou was still a young girl, so that her father could work as a machinist. They were poor, she was young and disabled and she was a victim at the hands of the very people who were supposed to care for her. These circumstances were hardly the healthiest for the young girl to grow up in, and it is not shocking that Betty Lou became increasingly unstable and inclined to criminality in such an environment during such a time of deprivation. However it is also noteworthy that many more people suffered equal or worse hardship, yet did not turn to criminal activity. Perhaps it was the combination of everything, all together at once, but as she grew up something was going very, very wrong inside Betty Lou.

At the age of fifteen she married her first husband, Robert Franklin Branson. Far from an age where anyone feels quite ready to move into adulthood, Betty Lou was married for the first time. She would remain with him for seventeen years before finally divorcing. Although she levied accusations of violence against all her husbands, Robert Franklin

Branson was the only one whose life she did not threaten directly herself. It appears he picked up where her father left off. If she was ever a unilateral victim, this may have been the one time. Within the first year she attempted suicide and became pregnant. They had a daughter together. She also later had a son with Robert Branson, who was also named Robert after his father. They went onto have four more children. Their children may have been a factor in reducing the marital violence, extending the duration of the relationship and, ultimately, saving Robert Branson Senior's life. In 1958 he evicted her from their home and put her on a bus to Virginia while he kept her children, at which point Betty again attempted suicide via an overdose of sleeping pills. They divorced in 1969, which left Betty Lou a financial and emotional wreck.

Being single took its toll on Betty Lou. She attached her self-worth to her ability to stay married. She began drinking to fight her feelings of loneliness. Between her own insecurities and the hard time she had getting money from either Robert Branson or the Welfare service to support her, Betty Lou soon felt she needed to remarry. She married Billy York Lane at the age of thirty two. Their marriage was a tumultuous one, and very short. There was evidence of mutual violence and disregard for each other's wellbeing. Lane had been abusive towards a previous partner and Betty Lou responded to his violence in turn. Her daughters recall how he used to beat her senseless and how she used to attack him. He initially wanted to charge her for attempted murder, but swiftly dropped the charges after he was forced to admit he had attacked her, broken her nose and threatened her life. They divorced the same year and remarried again shortly after the trial. After Betty Lou shot at him, Billy York Lane divorced her again, only a month after their remarriage, this time for good. It would prove the wisest decision of his life, as her subsequent husbands found out.

Betty Lou remained single for a year and unmarried for eight more years. During the interim Betty Lou worked in a warehouse, then took up work at a topless bar to cover the bills. She sent two of their children back home to Branson, as she could not afford to care for them. She went on to marry Ronnie C. Threlkold, her boyfriend of seven years, at the age of forty. However this relationship would be as unpredictable, violent and dangerous for Ronnie as it was for Billy. In this case there was little evidence Ronnie had been violent towards Betty Lou, although she accused him of violence at later dates, but her habits had been firmly cemented and she continued to display abusive behaviour towards him. She also continued to work at the topless bar, resulting in arrests and thirty days in country jail under the charge of public lewdness. Despite their seven year courtship, the marriage lasted just a year, culminating in Betty Lou Beets's attempted homicide of Ronnie in 1978, where she shot him in the stomach, wounding him, and their divorce in 1979.

She married Doyle Wayne Barker at the age of forty one, closely after her divorce from Threlkold. Their marriage lasted a mere seven weeks before her violent behaviour drove Doyle away from her. However his own violence was undeniable. He had stalked her, assaulted her and raped her during their short relationship. The day he left Betty Lou had bruises all over her face, neck, arms and chest. There is no available record of the divorce, however all living parties assumed it had taken place. However Doyle Wayne did not get out of their marriage unscathed. He disappeared after their divorce and his body was found years later, buried under a garage, killed by three gunshots.

But this grisly deed was not uncovered for many more years to come. Rather, Betty Lou went on to marry a firefighter named Jimmy Don Beets, her final husband, at the age of forty four.

"Jimmy Don Beets was a wonderful man," said a family friend. "He was loved by so many people. An old country boy that a lot people had respect for."

Their courtship would last a mere six months. Betty Lou would meet Jimmy while she worked as a waitress and the seduction began. Her two sons moved in with them. This would be her final marriage, and her actions within it would be her undoing. Although their courtship had been pleasant, they both suffered from alcoholism, which slowly drove their marriage to the same violence she had experienced previously. Less than a year later she murdered him by gunshot, and this time she was caught. Robert Branson, her son from her first marriage, had been informed that she intended to kill her last husband, telling him to steer clear of the residence as the murder took place. On the 6th of August 1983, Robert Branson Junior left their home and Betty Lou Beets committed the gruesome act. Not only did Robert provide evidence that the act was premeditated, but he also was expected to participate. Two hours after leaving the house, Robert Branson Junior returned, finding his step father dead with two gunshot wounds in his body. Rather than seek assistance, Robert Branson Junior, either tainted by a lifetime with a mother who viewed abuse and murder as daily events or himself an individual with low empathy, helped his mother to dispose of the body. Betty Lou Beets and Robert Branson Junior carted Jimmy Don Beets' body outside to an ornamental wishing well that stood in the front yard of their house. Undetected, they cast the body inside.

Then, Betty Lou returned to the house to cover up her acts. She called the police to report her husband missing from their Cedar Creek Lake home. The next day, Betty Lou became more devious. Perhaps inspired, perhaps unnerved by her success killing Doyle Wayne Barker, she realized she needed to create a story with which to divert the police from her trail. Robert Branson Junior recalled to the press how she had taken some of Jimmy Don Beets's heart medication down to his boat at the lake. Then she had removed the propeller, placed the medication in the boat and abandoned it, floating loosely in the water. Later that day, as the twenty four hours since Jimmy Don Beets's initial disappearance drew to a close, various officials began the search for the presumably missing man. Officers from the Henderson County Sheriff's department, various members of the fire department, as well as agents from the Texas Parks and Wildlife department searched for three weeks. They naturally found no body. However they did find Jimmy Don Beets's boat drifting in the lake, near to the Redwood Beach Marina. There they found his fishing license, an unused life jacket and the heart medication which Betty Lou Beets had placed there. Not knowing anything about the murder or the forged evidence, they brought Betty Lou Beets to the Marina as the sole witness, where she identified the boat and its contents as those of her husband. Although no body had been recovered, it was considered case closed.

Betty Lou Beets would have likely got away with both murders, were it not for confidential information given to the Henderson County Sheriff's Department two years later. The information suggested that Jimmy Don Beets had not disappeared innocently, and that his assumed death, with no body that had been found, may be the result of foul play. The evidence was enough that the cold case was reopened in Spring 1985. As their suspicions became stronger, the investigators were drawn to Betty Lou Beets, who was arrested on the 8th of June of 1985 and then booked into the Henderson County Jail. An officer on the case, Rick Rose, who had been in charge of her arrest warrant, secured a further warrant to search the Beets's home and lands, including the yard. Ultimately, they discovered Jimmy Don Beets's remains buried under the wishing well where he had been left two years prior. But another discovery would surface that would further disturb the case. Also in the back yard was a storage shed which could be moved. When the officers moved it, something compelled them to disturb the soil that had lain there several years. Perhaps it was some confidential evidence or perhaps it was just intuition, but it paid off when they discovered a second body. Doyle Wayne Barker, still missing, was buried there, with three bullets in his body. All five bullets matched the .38 caliber pistol which had been seized from their home after another incident of Betty Lou's violent outbursts. Thanks to the calls she had made the very day of his disappearance there was no room to argue that she had been abusing drugs or alcohol at the time, but there had been no physical evidence that suggested to detectives at the time that Jimmy Don had been abusing her when the incident took place. Her position was weak.

Faced with the evidence, Robert Branson Junior and his sister Shirley finally confessed to their awareness of the killings, as well as their hand in the crimes that had taken place. Not only had Betty Lou told her son about the murder, but she had also informed her daughter, by the Shirley Stegner and not living at the family home, that she planned on killing her husband. Shirley was motivated by her confession to also confess to her involvement in another crime. She told the detectives that she had been involved in the burial of Doyle Wayne Barker's body in October of 1981 after Betty Lou had shot him to death.

In an effort to make herself more likeable to the jury, Betty Lou Beets raised her history of domestic violence as an excuse for her violent behaviour, levying charges against all her prior husbands, as well as her father. However, this would be the first that anyone had heard of most of these charges. This may have been due to attitudes of the times, a desire to protect her children, or the apparently two-sided nature of most of these incidents, however the jury would not believe her claims. They were just too convenient. Instead, it was clear to them that Betty Lou Beets was an unstable and dangerous woman and the only connection between the five men she married and their violence. Whatever the situation was, her psychological well being was never considered during the trial. Despite the obvious impact her upbringing and life would have on her mental state and the fact that her actions up until that point were indicative of definite mental illness, the trial system of the time did not account for that.

Furthermore, the premeditated nature of her actions was evident through her children's abundant testimonials, where they confessed she had shared her intent to kill not only the husbands she managed to murder, but that she had expressed a desire to kill all the men she had been married to. Not only that, but her success concealing the bodies, under the wishing well and under the garden shed, showed a lack of remorse and serious consideration of her crimes. However it seems Betty Lou had not been as careful as she thought. As soon as the trial began, various other witnesses emerged to testify against her. Various people recalled her attempting to collect life insurance of over a hundred thousand dollars as well as a pension of over a thousand dollars a month after Jimmy Don's declared death. A year after the official death of Jimmy Don Beets, she successfully sold his boat, the primary evidence that he had disappeared. She claimed she did not know about his pension or insurance, however seeing as Jimmy Don Beets was already retired and claiming his pension, this claim fell short. Furthermore, had she no awareness of them she would not have pursued either so actively. She claimed she had been told about them when she visited an attorney by the name or E. Ray Andrews about a fire insurance claim she needed to make, at which point he discovered she could claim his insurance and pension. However her own filing for these benefits did not align with the supposed visit, and the only person who could say for sure that she had not known about her deceased husband's finances was E. Ray Andrews himself, who agreed to represent her in exchange for the rights to book and movie deals concerning her life and case.

Betty Lou Beets was indicted for murder for remuneration or the promise of remuneration, with her recovery of his life insurance and pension as evidence. She plead not guilty and was taken to trial, where she was found guilty of the capital offence of first degree murder on the 11th of October of 1985. She was found again guilty during a hearing on the 14th of October 1985 and was sentenced to death by the trial court. This was due to her prior history of violence and attempted murders, which suggested that she would present a threat to others in the future, specifically to any man who entered a relationship with her again. Yet her conviction and sentence were quickly and successfully appealed to the Texas Court of Criminal Appeals. Such was the situation that, under Texas law, crime for the sake of insurance and pension claims was not covered by the definition of "murder for remuneration", instead falling into two separate categories of first degree murder and insurance fraud, or crime with intent to commit insurance fraud. The Texas Court of Criminal Appeals reversed her conviction for capital murder, citing the Texas Penal Code as evidence that her particular case could not be filed as "murder for remuneration".

The State then requested a rehearing of the cause. Although her original conviction had been overturned, the fact remained that Betty Lou Beets was guilty of homicide under some circumstance or another.

On the 21st of September of 1988, the Court of Criminal Appeals reinstated her conviction and sentence based on the evidence received. Betty Lou Beets was on death row. Her execution was scheduled for the 8th of November 1989.

However her court case did not go as it should have in the first place. Attorney E. Ray Andrews was heavily invested in sensationalizing her case as much as he could, seeing as he would profit enormously from the case blowing up into a media phenomenon. So although she claimed and he later agreed that she had known nothing of her husband's finances, the trial was conducted under the assumption that she was fully aware of the money she would receive. Not only that, but E. Ray Andrews did everything in his power to create a more dramatic case on both sides, which ultimately meant excluding Betty Lou from much of the information about her own trial. Betty Lou was becoming desperate at this point. Although she had a long history of domestic violence, attempted murder and two bodies in her garden, she decided to attempt to blame the murder of Jimmy Don Beets on Robert Branson Junior, her own son. She did not seem to have made the statement in sound mind, but E. Ray Andrews allowed her to speak on her own behalf and did not retract it, as it added dramatic quality to the event. He tried to cover up later, saying that Betty Lou had possibly been taking the blame for her son, however he had no proof other than that Robert Branson Junior was male and from a rough background. This statement and its acceptance horrified the court, as it was alarming to them to see a mother who, rather than protect her children, was willing to throw them under the bus by falsely accusing them of a crime she had more than evidently committed. Furthermore, by admitting and adhering to the story that Robert Branson Junior was in fact the actual killer, Betty Lou lost all chances of arguing that she acted in self-defence and made her own accusations of domestic violence against Jimmy Don and her prior husbands completely irrelevant. This is despite the fact that a leading domestic violence specialist of the time believed Betty Lou Beets had been significantly mentally impacted by her experiences, and that she suffered "the emotional, cognitive, and behavioural components of battered woman syndrome, rape trauma syndrome, and PTSD" which he added must have interacted with her pre-existing organic brain damage from her childhood illness, history of battering and substance abuse. All together, this would have presented a robust case for her mental illness and need for treatment rather than punishment. However E. Ray Andrews discarded this option in favour of the more dramatic choice of supporting Betty Lou's accusation against her son. They became stuck in the position of having to argue she did not kill her husband at all. This context may have reduced her sentence, or made her eligible to claim insanity. However neither of these options were available.

Throughout the entire case, E. Ray Andrews failed to represent her seriously and did nothing to prevent her from shooting herself in the foot repeatedly. In fact, seeing the case was a lost cause and that he stood to gain more from her sentence than her freedom, Andrews began drinking heavily for the duration of the trial. He chose not to bear witness to her claims that she did not know about Jimmy Don Beets's pension or insurance, which would have transformed the case to one of murder in the context of domestic violence, rather than murder for remuneration. He managed to offer the jury no reasons to consider that Betty Lou was not a serious threat to those around her, eventually sealing her fate. Yet he remained her attorney for the duration of her appeal as well. It was he who raised the point that her financial gain was not necessarily the motivator for murder, but a by product. He also finally raised that she was not aware of the insurance or pension until she spoke to him, however this was met with scepticism due to his negligence to mention it any sooner, and was perceived as a lie in effort to overturn Betty Lou's criminal charges after his initial failure to protect her.

On the 16th of October 1989, Betty Lou filed a motion called a stay of execution which would delay her execution to give her time to prepare and file a habeas corpus application with the state. On the 1st of November she filed the application and the trial court delayed her execution so that the claims she was raising, such as consideration towards her mental state and marital conditions, could be properly addressed. During this time Betty Lou wrote several letters from prison in which she attempted to defend her good name and that of her last husband. She attempted to balance the accusations that she was a black widow by reminding the court that she was Jimmy Don's fourth wife as well. However his previous wives did not come forward to support her. She also defended her own identity, denying that she ever worked as a barmaid, regardless of her own charges for lewd behaviour, and that she was never on welfare, despite her claims after her first divorce. She also said that the Fire Department Chaplain, who stated he had informed her about Beets's insurance and pension, had spoken to her sister in law, Betty Beets, instead. She even quibbled over the descriptions of her garden, insisting the well was a planter in the shape of a well and not an actual well. It was clear that Betty Lou Beets was desperate to save face and project a more pleasant, more ordinary identity than the one which E. Ray Andrews had created for her in the courtroom. It was also clear that her mental health was degrading as she endured life in prison and submitted her habeas corpus petition. In her petition she argued against her sentence of the death penalty, raising issues such as the alleged value Jimmy Don Beets apparently added the community, the testimonials of victims and sufferers whose statements were unconstitutional under the Victim Impact Statements act of 1987, and the poor assistance which E. Ray Andrews provided, especially regarding her history of domestic abuse. Yet without his help in writing and presenting the letter, her claims were weak and not fully backed by legal evidence. Andrews did not visit her from the point of her sentencing and prepared for her trials without ever speaking to her. Furthermore, she could have claimed that his services were provided against American Bar Association rules, which prohibit the trade of legal services for copyright issues, such as the rights to her case. None of this was raised by her against him, and as such it was not considered during her habeas corpus appeal.

However on the 27th of June her appeal for state habeas corpus was turned away. She was placed in the position of proving that, had E. Ray Andrews presented a testimony about her lack of awareness of the insurance and her history of domestic violence, the jury would have judged her not guilty of a capital crime. Without a proper attorney to defend her, it would be impossible for Betty Lou to prove this was the case, and the court deemed Andrews's mistakes to have been harmless to her trial. The Fifth Circuit Court of Appeals went on to turn down her final appeals. The judges remained convinced that, regardless of any remaining evidence, Betty Lou Beets's history of violence and attempted murder, along with the two concealed bodies in her garden, were evidence enough that a death sentence was a fair response to the crime that had taken place. She had displayed violence her whole life, even towards men who had not presented a threat to her, and had attempted to kill all but one of her husbands. She had concealed her murders carefully and for many years and was willing to place the blame on her own adult son. In other words, regardless of her own situation, her criminal intent was viewed as evident and incorrigible, and her death sentence was the only fitting end to her crime spree.

On death row, Betty Lou Beets retained some supporters, mostly her own children. Some of Betty Lou's daughters went to E. Ray Andrews with photographic evidence of the domestic abuse she had suffered in order to request a parole review, but were declined. They insisted on presenting the evidence that she had suffered and that her acts of violence were a result of brain damage and abuse, not of malicious intent. Faye Lane, one of her daughters, insisted that her mother would only have done anything so horrific if she believed she was abused. Domestic violence awareness groups and charities acting against the death sentence appealed to have her sentence changed to a life sentence in prison, based not only on her own suffering, but on their universal stance against the irreversible process of the death penalty. Yet even those defending her maintained that she was a violent, unpredictable woman and not safe to exit into the general public.

And not all her children were so kind. Shirley told the press that Doyle Wayne Barker was killed because he owned the trailer where they lived, and that after the divorce which Barker had initiated, Betty Lou and her children would be evicted from the trailer and left homeless. This set a precedent where even her own daughter could not believe that Betty Lou was completely unaware of the financial benefits of murdering Jimmy Don Beets, especially not after she had successfully killed Barker. Knowing that she was still doubted and seeing hope as ever distant, Betty Lou composed her memoirs from death row, presenting her case.

Beets turned to her last resort which was to appeal to then-governor George W. Bush to spare her life. After a media incident where he jokingly insulted the last woman to be executed in Texas in an insensitive manner, George W. Bush seemed keen to prove he had no bias against women, even in the prison system, and agreed to review her case. This would have meant hearing the witnesses which had not been heard by the trial lawyer and present a case against her execution based on the circumstances of her life, including medical and psychiatric evidence. He could have granted her a thirty day reprieve in which he made his decision, however this never materialized. His number was made available and he received thousands of calls and letters from people urging him to spare her, with only fifty seven endorsing her sentence. Yet he did not grant the reprieve or halt the execution.

Betty Lou Beets was finally executed on the 24th of February of 2000, via lethal injection. Protestors from various organisations gathered outside as her sentence awaited. She declined both her last meal and her final statement, having been given by then enough time to make sense of what was happening and to say everything which needed to be said. Strapped to the death chamber gurney, she received her injection at six pm and died within eighteen minutes. She was sixty two years old. She left behind five adult children, nine grandchildren and six great-grandchildren, as well as her memoirs. Her story may be shocking, and it may be hard to pick sides at times, but that is exactly why her trial presents a solid case against the black and white ideals the court system held regarding crime and punishment, perpetrator and victim, defence and offence. Someone can at once be a victim of horrific crimes and a perpetrator of them, at once be a defendant and raise accusations, at once deserve punishment yet suffer a crime gone unpunished. There is no doubt that Betty Lou Beets was a violent woman who invited violence into her own life, an alcoholic and a murderer. However there is no doubt either that she was a good mother within her capacity, a victim of a series of horrific crimes, a disabled person with a background she could not escape and a desperate woman who saw no way out of her situation. Neither black nor white, good not bad, Betty Lou Beets sits in the grey areas of the law.

KILLER CRYSTAL MAE WAGNER

47

ANA BENSON

History shows us that men are most likely to commit heinous crimes but women are no strangers to violence either. Yes, they do not kill frequently and female killers do not engage in killing sprees so often. Instead, their crimes are driven by passion and sometimes even obsession with another person. They are not prone to selecting a random victim but would turn on their partners, friends, or family. Women are usually not killing for the thrill but they do so for their own personal gain, even if it seems illogical to a bystander. So as you may already know, whenever a body turns up somewhere, the police would immediately question the closest family members.

Crystal Mae Wagner's case is intriguing because she managed to include a third man into the whole narrative and make him do the dirty job for her. The overly brutal killing and the disposal of the body shocked the Bibb County in Georgia. Luckily, Crystal Mae Wagner's body count didn't escalate and she was caught in time. But the trial and the analysis of her psychological profile intrigued everyone who was involved in this case. What makes a loving mother turn on her husband? And was there something that pushed her over the edge to seek help from her lover in order to do this gruesome murder? Let's dive in deeper into this case and discover more details about Crystal Mae Wagner and her life.

Early life

Crystal Mae Wagner (née Carver) was born in 1980 and grew up with her grandparents, mother, and an uncle. The Carvers were a tight family that kept to themselves but remained close to their relatives who were living in the same area. The identity of Crystal Mae's father was unknown. However, a rumor that her uncle is her actual father kept circulating among the neighbors. Crystal Mae was diagnosed with rheumatoid arthritis at a very young age and this horrible illness will leave a permanent mark on her physique. This is an autoimmune disease that makes your own body turn on itself and destroy the tissue. She was left with physical deformities on her joints and skin.

Crystal Mae's childhood wasn't easy at all. Besides rheumatoid arthritis that caused great pain to her body, she was also physically and mentally abused by her family members. She would often be ignored and left to take care of herself without any help from those who were closest to her. The feeling of loneliness would be predominant in her early life and she desperately needed someone who would make her feel wanted. She felt like her family didn't need her at all and that she was unwelcome in her own home. On the other hand, she was often locked in the house and was forbidden from going out. Crystal Mae had no friends which undoubtedly took a toll on her mental state. Her views on emotional relationships were influenced by the lack of affection she got from her mother and grandparents. Crystal Mae was certain that the only way to attract someone is to act like "a piece of meat" and do anything that was asked of her even if she didn't feel like it.

So when Crystal Mae met her future husband, she saw him as the way out of the abusive and loveless environment she grew up in. It didn't matter that Bobby Gene Wagner was seven years older than her. Crystal Mae loved the attention she was getting from him and felt like she finally belonged somewhere. Bobby Gene Wagner had a steady job and he was capable of supporting Crystal Mae. The pair got married soon after and they had a son. But things got a bit rocky after some time. Crystal Mae and Bobby Gene decided to take some time off and see other people. She was only twenty-two years old and wanted to explore different things after gaining her independence.

Crystal Mae Wagner met Shay Alan Morey while she was estranged from her husband. They were the same age and clicked almost immediately. Their romance blossomed quickly and he accepted Crystal Mae's son as his own. However, Crystal Mae Wagner got back together with her husband and the family was back together. She continued to see Shay Alan Morey every now and then. It seems like Bobby Gene Wagner was oblivious to his wife's affair even though he met Shay Alan Morey and the two of them would end up spending a lot of time together.

The couple moved into a south Macon motel called Travel Inn which is located near the Interstate 475. Their son lived with them as well. Shay Alan Morey would join them in the motel but he was in a separate room. Bobby Gene Wagner was certain that Morey was still just a friend and that he was helping Crystal Mae with the toddler. Bobby Gene worked at Heart of Georgia Towing Company and he was really well liked there. He was an excellent employee that never complained and truly enjoyed his job. Bobby Gene Wagner loved both Crystal Mae and their little boy so he was very happy to provide them with everything they needed. He even tried to find Shay Alan Morey a position at the firm and help him get his life back on track.

Unfortunately, the situation between the three of them would turn sour pretty quickly and Bobby Gene Wagner would end up dead. There were no signs that could have warned Bobby Gene on what was about to unfold in their motel room.

The murder

Crystal Mae Wagner and Shay Alan Morey talked about the murder at least a couple of days prior to the crime itself. They discussed everything in detail and made a quick plan that involved the exact manner of the killing and the body disposal site. What prompted Crystal Mae Wagner to start thinking about eliminating her husband is still unclear but her relatives would later say that she felt like she had no freedom in the marriage and that the fact that she was tied down to one man was suffocating her. So she confided in her lover who was willing to do the dirty work for her in order to prove his devotion and love. Crystal Mae didn't even consider getting a divorce and though that the only way she could be with Shay Alan Morey was to completely erase Bobby Gene from her life.

The plan was to get Bobby Gene Wagner into the motel room's bathroom with the story that the entire family is invited to a birthday party and that he needed to get ready as soon as possible. Shay Alan Morey would enter the bathroom and murder Bobby Gene quickly and without making a huge mess. Crystal Mae was certain that the best way to hide Bobby Gene's corpse is to tie him down to a heavy object and submerge him in the water. The police would later discover cinder blocks and cables stashed in both the motel room and Crystal Mae's vehicle.

But even the best plans do fail somewhere along the way and this happened in the murder of Bobby Gene Wagner as well. It was February the 10th 2005 when Bobby Gene Wagner entered the bathroom. His wife told him to get cleaned up because they will be visiting some family friends. Shay Alan Morey waited outside and as soon as Crystal Mae gave him the signal, he burst into the bathroom and started beating Bobby Gene who was in the shower. He was clearly startled and didn't fight back. Even though Shay Alan Morey injured him badly, Bobby Gene was still alive and conscious. He was bleeding and had visible bruises all over his body but that didn't prevent him from going back to his room and telling Crystal Mae what happened. He asked her to call the ambulance and the police because he was attacked. Crystal Mae ignored him and the couple went back to the bathroom together. She left the bathroom and went straight to Shay Alan Morey's room to inform him that her husband is calling the police.

Shay Alan Morey quickly returned to the scene of the crime and launched himself on Bobby Gene. He stabbed him straight into the heart, delivering the fatal blow that left Bobby Gene dead on the spot. The lovers started to panic because it was obvious that it would be very difficult to carry out Bobby Gene's corpse from the motel without being seen. Plus, Bobby Gene was a large man and Shay Alan Morey was simply not strong enough to do it on his own. Therefore, his only option was to dismember Bobby Gene's body and load him up in the car once piece at the time. It is also important to mention that Crystal

Mae's and Bobby Gene's two-year-old son was present in the room while all of this was happening, including the murder of his father.

The plans to go to a river or a lake with the cinder blocks fell through and Shay Alan Morey decided to leave the body behind an abandoned house that was rarely visited by anyone living in the area. He tried to conceal Bobby Gene Wagner's identity by burning his face but left plenty of clues on the spot. Morey didn't stop there but tried to pile up various garbage and aluminum construction pieces on top of the corpse. However, his behavior on the disposal site was unorganized and even left the tools he used back in the motel in order to cut up Bobby Gene's lifeless body.

The discovery of the body

Even though the location that was chosen by Shay Alan Morey was remote and pretty secluded, it took only four days for Bobby Gene's body to be discovered. The first clue that something was wrong was the fact that Bobby Gene Wagner failed to show up at his workplace on the day after the murder. His boss, Robert Allen Wagner called him several times but got no answer. He knew that Bobby Gene sometimes talked about his rocky marriage so he drove to the motel in order to see if everything was alright. Robert Allen Wagner noticed that Bobby Gene's car was parked in the parking lot in front of the motel so he expected to find him in his room. He knocked on the door for a couple of minutes but nobody answered.

Robert Allen Wagner gave up and decided to return the next day. The second try was successful and he was greeted by Shay Alan Morey. Crystal Mae and her son stood behind him in the doorway. They told Robert that Bobby Gene suddenly decided to go to Florida. Robert could see that the motel room was chaotic and that the clothes and trash were all over the place. He would later tell the law enforcement: "That room was a total mess. The odor was so bad I could hardly go in." In the meantime, the authorities discovered Bobby Gene Wagner's body in Twiggs County. The scene was horrifying because the body was dismembered and burned by fire. They managed to find Bobby Gene's wallet that had his ID card inside and a letter with his current place of residence. They discovered his cellphone nearby as well. They checked the call list for his number and saw that he tried to contact the sheriff's office on the 10th of February.

Due to the nature of this crime, the detectives were certain that someone who was close to Bobby Gene Wagner was the perpetrator. They immediately drove to the motel and found the room he was staying in with his wife and child. Crystal Mae Wagner was in there and she appeared to be shocked when the investigators told her that they have discovered her husband's remains. She repeated the Florida story but when the detectives presented her with their own timeline that included the exact date of the call to the sheriff's office, she made a claim that she was sleeping in their motel room while the crime was being committed. Crystal Mae Wagner also mentioned that she drank "a sleeping potion" that knocked her out completely and she couldn't register what was going on around her. Her second statement did not include the so-called sleeping potion so it was obvious to the detectives that Crystal Mae was lying.

Crystal Mae Wagner and Shay Alan Morey were arrested while they were attempting to pick up Bobby Gene Wagner's last paycheck. The scene itself was quite traumatic because both of them were crying and were visibly upset. Department of Family and Children Services picked up Crystal Mae's two-year-old boy. Crystal Mae Wagner's story was filled with holes and she finally pointed her finger in the right direction. She told the detectives who were working on the case that Shay Alan Morey was the killer. However, she also added that Morey was threatening to murder her and her son if she turned him to the authorities. That was the way to justify the fact that she lied to the detectives in her previous statements. She was arrested five days after the murder and Bibb County was getting ready for the trial of both Crystal Mae Wagner and Shay Alan Morey.

The investigation and Morey's trial

The authorities immediately knew the identity of their victim but they needed to get a couple of things straight regarding the crime scene. Since they had both Shay Alan Morey and Crystal Mae Wagner in the custody, they headed straight to the motel room at the Travel Inn. After thorough testing, they concluded that the murder took place in the bathroom and the bathtub was used in order to drain the blood and reduce the possible mess during the dismemberment of the murder victim. The crime itself was starting to look grislier than they thought at first.

Crystal Mae Wagner stopped denying her knowledge about the crime but she stood by the claim that her life and the life of her baby boy were in danger if she told the authorities what happened. She even said to the detectives that she was present when Shay Alan Morey was purchasing the tools he would later on use for cutting up Bobby Gene Wagner's body. She sat in the car while Shay Alan loaded up a hatchet and a mallet into the trunk. She told the investigators that he choose Twiggs County as the location for body disposal because it is quite rural but the detectives were a bit skeptical about this claim. Crystal Mae's grandmother lived close by so the spot was probably chosen because she knew about it prior to the murder and could provide Shay Alan Morey with the directions on how to get there.

The police investigators started digging deeper into the lives of both the victim and the perpetrators. A large number of witnesses that included friends and relatives of both Crystal Mae and Bobby Gene talked to the authorities and filled up the holes in the story that painted a picture of an abusive marriage.

After speaking to Bobby Gene's friends and family, they discovered that the marriage between him and Crystal Mae was troubled from the very beginning. Bobby Gene Wagner had a tendency to fall for difficult women and all of his previous relationships were off and on. So when the two of them met, the pattern was repeated. Bobby Gene was an alcoholic and was very loud when he was drunk, but his friends and family loved him for his eagerness to help and be there for everyone when he was clean and sober. The couple got married when Crystal Mae was twenty-one years old back in 2001 and they soon got a baby boy who became the focus of Bobby Gene's attention. He was a hard worker before but he took extra hours in order to provide his son with everything he might need. However, his boss at Heart of Georgia Towing Company did notice that Bobby Gene Wagner was reluctant to go home after work and would often stay at the headquarters. When his boss tried talking to him about it, Bobby Gene told him that Crystal Mae was behaving erratically and that he was afraid for his life. He even mentioned to one friend that Crystal Mae tried to poison him on one occasion. Bobby Gene filed for a divorce one year after the birth of their baby.

Crystal Mae Wagner met Shay Alan Morey during that time and the two started a relationship. Bobby Gene Wagner wanted to get back together with his estranged wife for the sake of their child so he made a decision to forget and forgive everything that Crystal Mae put him through in the past. His only goal was to try and provide the best possible future for his baby boy. On the other hand, Crystal Mae wasn't ready to let go of her lover and he stayed in the picture. The investigators weren't able to pinpoint the motive for this murder at first and they were as confused as everyone else. But Shay Alan Morey started talking soon after the arrest and confessed that Crystal Mae told him that the only way they could be together was to eliminate Bobby Gene from their lives. He also told them that Crystal Mae was the perpetrator and that she attacked her husband in the bathroom. The story itself got even more confusing at this point because the detectives knew that they had the right people in the custody but the events were still unclear.

The investigators who were talking to Crystal Mae Wagner immediately noticed that her hands were very deformed. She told them about her illness and that she suffered from rheumatoid arthritis. Her hands were simply not strong enough for her to deliver the fatal blow to her husband or use a hatchet in order to dismember a body in a bathtub. As a matter of fact, her fingers and joints were disfigured. Therefore, the detectives knew that the only person who could have physically attack Bobby Gene Wagner was Shay Alan Morey. The case itself was becoming very solid and the investigators were certain that they had a good case against the lovers.

Shay Alan Morey was put to trial first. After all, he was the one who attacked and murdered Bobby Gene Wagner. Since the detectives managed to collect numerous evidence, including the murder weapon, the hearings didn't last a long time. Shay Alan Morey continued to claim that Crystal Mae Wagner was behind the murder and that she knew exactly what he was doing. As a matter of fact, Crystal Mae was pulling all the strings while he was simply "the muscle". He didn't deny that he was involved. Shay Alan Morey pleaded guilty to the murder of Bobby Gene Wagner in March of 2006, just thirteen months after the crime. He received a life sentence without the possibility of the parole. Morey was visibly upset when the judge delivered the sentence and his emotions got the best of him. He wept and cried as he was led out of the courtroom. Bibb County police force started gathering up the evidence for the second trial because it was time to prosecute Crystal Mae Wagner who was, after all, the one who came up with the plan to murder her husband.

The trial of Crystal Mae

Crystal Mae Wagner was expected to receive a death penalty but she gave up her right to a trial in front of a jury. It was a smart move by her defense team because they knew that she would have been found guilty. Instead, all witnesses were called to talk in front of a judge. Crystal Mae's team consisted of Frank Hogue and Laura D. Hogue. Their case relied heavily on the fact that Crystal Mae was abused as a child. After a psychological evaluation, a doctor discovered that she did have the abandonment issues and that Crystal needed someone to be with her at all times. She loved the attention and the fact that two men were fighting for her affections did bring out the worst out of her.

Bobby Gene Wagner's friends told a different story. Even though Crystal Mae had physical disabilities, she was very abusive towards her husband. The prosecution unsealed the divorce documents from 2004 and discovered a number of disturbing details that painted a different picture of Crystal Mae. Bobby Gene told his divorce attorneys that Crystal Mae was a violent drug abuser. Crystal Mae fired back and accused Bobby Gene of trying to choke her. Since Bobby Gene was physically stronger than Crystal Mae, her story sounded more believable. James Davis who was Bobby Gene Wagner's attorney during the divorce hearings told the judge that Bobby Gene confessed to him off the records that Crystal Mae would start the violence by attacking him first and he simply couldn't let her assault him without fighting back. Bobby Gene would later admit to the domestic violence and he was put on a probation in 2004. The couple got back together that same year and Crystal Mae retracted her story.

A couple of Bobby Gene's friends took the stand and told the judge about the relationship between the accused and the victim. Howard Schurter knew Bobby Gene for years and he even moved into Bobby Gene's old trailer which he shared with Crystal Mae at one time. He told the court that Bobby Gene would often leave things in the trailer because he wanted to keep them hidden from Crystal Mae. A lot of his personal documents and the divorce papers were left in Schurter's trailer. Jason Tanner used to live with Bobby Gene Wagner and knew the man pretty well. He described him as someone who had a big heart but would always end up with a wrong kind of women. Bobby Gene Wagner had a failed marriage in the past. He was involved with a woman called Michelle from Kentucky back in the 1990s. He really hoped that his second marriage would be different. Jason Tanner also added: "He was just trying to find somebody to love him. And he wanted to take care of his kid. That man worked 16 hours a day."

Escaping an abusive partner is very difficult regardless of a gender and William Smith who used to work with Bobby Gene Wagner at Precision Tune confirmed that Bobby Gene was in fear for his own life even years before the murder occurred. He told the judge that Bobby Gene would sometimes complain to his co-workers that his wife is going to kill him but would act like nothing was wrong only a couple of days later. When Crystal Mae's relatives took the stand, they were on her side, confirming the story of the abuse and neglect that she suffered in her youth. Marsha Mathews who is closely related to Crystal Mae Wagner did not support her innocence but was listed as her witness. She did her best to shed some light on the motive itself even though she didn't get a chance to speak in front of a judge. She said the following to the reporters: "I feel she felt trapped over the years." It seemed like Crystal Mae Wagner wanted to get out of her marriage with Bobby Gene Wagner and instead of filing for a divorce, she decided to involve her lover. The lead prosecutor Elizabeth Bobbitt also presented a crucial piece of evidence – a letter written by Crystal Mae to Shay Alan Morey in which she discusses the details of the murder.

Crystal Mae Wagner pleaded guilty to murder on 17th of March 2010, ending a long trial process. Just like Shay Alan Morey, she was sentenced to life in prison. Crystal Mae Wagner was tearful during the entire course of the sentencing and broke down when the judge delivered the verdict. She is serving her sentence at the moment and will not be eligible for a parole. Bobby Gene's and Crystal Mae's son was taken in by his maternal grandmother.

KILLER TEEN NIKKI REYNOLDS

It is not often that stories appear where we find the perpetrators of violence being children and the victims being parents. Although, scattered throughout history it has been seen that children can be capable of shocking amounts of violence, and many, assuming their innocent nature, fall victim to them. In Coral Springs, Florida in 1997 one such story took place. And still the actions of the evening resonate throughout the community.

In The Beginning

Born in 1979 to a mother that didn't want her, Jacquiline "Nikki" Reynolds was adopted by Robert and Billie Jean Reynolds three months after her birth. The Reynolds were a loving, Christian family from Coral Springs, Florida and they were delighted to welcome their new daughter into their lives.

There was nothing that they wouldn't do for Nikki. Robert Reynolds worked for the Department of Transportation and Billie Jean was an administrative assistant at RJ Reynolds. They had a quiet home and they were devoted to making their daughter happy.

Nikki was a good child. She was devoted to the church, like her parents, and she loved her parents deeply. She would go to the mall with her mother or watch baseball games with her father. She could never spend too much time with them. The Reynolds did everything to ensure that Nikki was being raised in a loving and non-judgmental environment.

Friends and family would agree that the environment was loving, but the Reynolds gave Nikki everything she wanted. She was pampered, she was spoiled, and in the end, she was a bit of a brat. Sometimes the best intentions can have the worst consequences.

Still, Nikki, as she got older, became a good student and didn't act out. She achieved good grades in school and went out of her way to become involved in extra curricular activities. She also stayed heavily involved with the church alongside her parents.

By all appearances, Nikki was the perfect child. She was the child that most parents dream of having and Robert and Billie Jean were delighted with her. But children grow up, despite anything that their parents try to do to stop it, and Nikki was no exception. And not all children grow up in a manner that their parents can be proud of.

The Beginning of the End

Nikki went from being the model child to what most people would call a 'troubled teen'. It didn't start in the way one would expect, with failing grades and a lack of interest in school. It started with a lie, and one that shocked family and friends in the disturbing nature of it.

In 1996, sixteen-year-old Nikki came home from school and claimed that she had been assaulted after getting off of the school bus. Naturally her parents were shocked and appalled to hear that this had happened to her. They immediately called the police to handle the situation officially. Nikki claimed she had been attacked by someone she knew, at first. But when questioned by the police her story quickly changed.

She went on to say that she didn't know her attacker and then that the attack hadn't happened at all. She hadn't been raped. She'd made the whole story up.

Now why would a sixteen-year-old, devote Christian girl make up a story about being raped? Why would she go to the extreme of telling her parents and getting the police involved if it was just a story?

It turns out that Nikki hadn't been raped. Rather she was in a relationship, the first one of a sexual nature in her lifetime, and she was terrified to tell her parents about it. She was worried about what they would think about their daughter sacrificing her morals and her principles just to have a boyfriend. But Carlos Infante was her entire world. The sixteen-year-old classmate was consuming her life focus to the point that she hadn't hesitated to throw caution to the wind.

And when the thought of telling her parents about what was going on had come up, in her mind, fabricating a rape story had seemed like a better idea. Nikki was also concerned that she might be pregnant, a worry that was quickly put to rest, but it also influenced her decision to pursue the rape narrative.

Billie Jean was extremely unhappy with Nikki, potentially for the first time during her parenting of the girl. She didn't like the fact that Nikki had a boyfriend. She didn't like the fact that she'd sacrificed her principles and morals, the beliefs that they thought they'd instilled into her all for some boy. They believed that they'd raised a good, Christian girl and for the first time they were starting to question that belief.

Bille Jean and Robert disliked the idea of Nikki having a boyfriend, it didn't particularly matter who he was. They viewed it as a step down for her. They saw it as a complete abandonment of her belief system, something they had strived to instill in her over the course of her entire life. She was sacrificing everything in order to be with this boy, from their point of view. She was losing herself in him. And Billie Jean and Robert wanted to help get Nikki back on a clear path, on a Christian path.

So, they insisted that she spend less time with Carlos and more time with the church. They hoped that in doing so she would see her wrongdoings and find her true self again. They hoped that in spending more time with the church that she would become closer to the family again and forget about Carlos.

Billie Jean believed that Nikki needed to spend more time with a better group of people, a Christian group of people. She hoped that if Nikki spent time around other good, Christian kids that she would find her way again, that she would find a better crowd. And Billie Jean was willing to go to great lengths to ensure that her daughter found a path that fit with the beliefs and morals of the family.

But sometimes the child, no matter how much they push, cannot realize the hopes and dreams of parents. And sometimes, despite all efforts, things still go wrong.

Rebellion Continues

Teenage rebellion can be a strong force, however, and the more that Billie Jean pushed Nikki to go to church the more she resisted. Nikki said, "I knew that the way I was living was not right in God's eyes, but I did not want to hear all of that." She was too engulfed in her life with Carlos. He was quickly becoming her entire world and nothing else mattered to her. Not her parents, and certainly not her church.

The rebellion was extending into her school life. Nikki, who had once been a good student with marks that her parents could be proud of was now beginning to skip class. Her grades were beginning to fall as a result and she was no longer the academic force that she was before.

It was to the point that Billie Jean and Robert barely recognized the girl that they had raised anymore. Who was this young woman living in their house? She reflected none of the morals and principles they had raised her to uphold. She wouldn't listen to them. She opposed them at every turn. They began to wonder what had happened to their daughter Nikki. Where had she gone?

Nikki went from a happy-go-lucky child that was a pleasure to be around, a child who was soft spoken and loved to go to church to a girl no one could recognize. She wore dark clothes, she changed her music, she changed her bedroom to dark colours – she became the opposite of herself. It was hard to tell if this was simply teenage rebellion or something more going on. Was this all because of Carlos or was there some deeper problem at play?

She slept a lot, more than any teenager should and she isolated herself from her family. Gone were the days of ice cream and base ball games. She no longer went on trips to the mall with her mother. She no longer went to church with her family. She became disinterested in many things that used to hold her attention, things that used to captivate her. Her whole world now revolved around Carlos.

It was her first sexual relationship with anyone in her life and it had reached the point of obsession. She filled her diary with everything to do with Carlos. Her room was plastered with photos of him. Her every waking moment revolved around him. There was an unnatural intensity to her emotions towards him, an unhealthy intensity. And it was quickly becoming evident that this was a problem.

Naturally, Billie Jean and Robert were very concerned about their daughter's current mental state. She was not herself, and the only thing they could blame was Carlos as he was the only changing factor in her life. It seemed that he was a negative influence on Nikki in many ways. He didn't make good grades as a student, and now her grades were plummeting as well.

Billie Jean was also worried that he was coming over every day, potentially when they were at work. They had no way to confirm this, but she didn't like the idea that he was at the house alone with her while they were at work. It didn't sit well with her.

So Billie Jean put her foot down, perhaps for the first time in her experience as a parent. She began to tell Nikki no, especially when it came to Carlos. And Nikki handled it with the maturity level of a toddler as opposed to that of a teenager. Nikki threw awful tantrums. Billie Jean and Nikki would engage in screaming matches in the house that would result in slammed doors. The result was very wearing on Billie Jean. She found herself screaming at Nikki almost all of the time. This was not what she wanted her life as a mother to be. This was not the girl she had raised. She needed to do something about this, but she was at a loss as to what the solution could be.

And despite the screaming matches and the orders to stay away, Nikki still kept seeing Carlos. It seemed that nothing could keep her from Carlos. She would sneak out at night when everyone was asleep to see him and it didn't matter what the consequences were.

Billie Jean's frustration escalated to the point that one day she confided in a friend saying "Don't be surprised if one day you come home and there's police cars and fire trucks up and down the street 'cause one of us, it'll be me or Nikki, but one of us will be gone."

Billie Jean's prediction would prove to hit a little too close to home in the coming days. And the aftermath would shock everyone.

Intervention

It was May 14, 1997 when the school counselor contacted Billie Jean to tell her that there was trouble with Nikki and Carlos. She asked that Billie Jean come in and speak with her in person and that Billie Jean, Robert, and Nikki come in for a full meeting the next day. Upon visiting the high school, the counselor told Billie Jean that Nikki and Carlos had more than just the usual high school relationship issues to deal with.

That day Nikki had told the counselor that she was pregnant with Carlos' baby. This had naturally prompted the counselor to contact Billie Jean immediately about the issue. Billie Jean, having already dealt with Nikki's questionable honesty with the previous rape accusation, was hesitant to believe the pregnancy claim. She was fairly certain that this was another one of Nikki's schemes, but there was a sure way to determine its legitimacy.

So she took Nikki to the drug store to find out what was what.

The results of the pregnancy test were negative. That didn't mean Billie Jean was any less pleased with her daughter. Nikki called Carlos with the news. And despite having a counseling meeting the next day Billie Jean decided to seek guidance from a higher power. She dragged Nikki away from the phone and took Nikki to see the church counselor.

Nikki spoke with her pastor as they waited to see the counselor. He was supportive as he talked to her about her boyfriend problems and offered her guidance. Their conversation with the counselor did not have the same supportive tone. The counselor spent the session telling Nikki that her mother did not deserve the behaviour she was displaying. She raised her voice and yelled at Nikki. This didn't go over very well.

Nikki removed herself from the office and from the church. She wanted nothing more to do with the impromptu counseling session. And as she stood in the parking lot of the church she even debated removing herself from the family by running away. But she didn't run away, however. Instead, she took a higher ground, something that hadn't been seen from her in almost a year. She went back into the counselor's office and apologized to her mother. And she finished the session with the counselor before returning home with her mother.

Billie Jean believed that they had made a step in the right direction. She would be the one to learn how wrong she was about that fact.

Confusion and Confessions

It was barely an hour after their visit to the counselor on May 14, 1997 that the call came in to 911. At 7:07pm Nikki Reynolds' panicked voice came over the phone saying "I stabbed her repeatedly in the back. There's blood all over her and all over the floor and everything."

Police were at her house in minutes and the scene that they witnessed was one that would stay with some of the officers for years after. When police arrived they found Nikki waiting on her doorstep. One of the officers who responded indicated that "She had blood all over, blood on her legs, blood on her face."

Nikki was placed in the back of the police car and left to wait while the police went to investigate. A tape recorder was left on with her in the police car so that anything that was said while she was alone was recorded and on file. It recorded her praying that her mother was still be alive and saying that she had learned her lesson. She was asking God to forgive her and for her mother to please still be alive.

Her mother was brought out of the house on a stretcher by the EMTs and she was still alive at the time that she left the house. However, Billie Jean was pronounced dead at the hospital at 8:10pm after suffering from 13 stab wounds.

Nikki was taken to the police department immediately. Robert came home from work to find the house in a state of chaos, surrounded by police cars and police tape. He hadn't yet been informed of the situation that had come to pass behind the front doors of his home. He broke down at the news that his wife was gone and that his daughter was responsible. The shock of it was something that he couldn't quite comprehend.

The scene inside the house was gruesome and shocking to police investigators. It depicted Billie Jean's terrible, drawn out death as she fought to get away from her daughter. But there was no escape for her as she was stabbed repeatedly until she finally lay immobile on the floor.

The police found the kitchen knife that had been used as the murder weapon in the sink and it still had blood on it. They also found evidence that someone, likely Nikki, had attempted to clean up the scene using towels and dishcloths. The blood soaked pieces of cloth were scattered about the kitchen unable to handle the sheer amount of blood that had resulted from the incident.

While the police officers worked diligently at the crime seen the detectives questioned Nikki about the murder. And it didn't take too much effort to get her to talk.

"I didn't have any intentions of lying." Nikki said. "I didn't have any secrets. I wanted to get it out." She felt almost compelled to tell the story of what had happened. She needed to let them know.

"It was simple, all I had to ask her was what happened today and just started chatting. She went through the whole story from a to b," said the detective who interviewed Nikki.

The story that was told by Nikki revolved heavily around Carlos Infante, the infamous boyfriend. Nikki had used her fake pregnancy to keep Carlos in a relationship with her when he wanted to leave, fearing what would happen if he left. When she had found out she was not pregnant, for sure, she called him to give the news. Carlos indicated that he wanted nothing to do with her and all of her lies. He'd had enough. Billie Jean had even got on the phone with Carlos and apologized for all of the drama that he'd had to endure at the hands of her daughter.

Nikki had decided then and there that someone would die that day. She even took a handful of aspirin before going to the counseling meeting with her mother at the church. She was certain that she could overdose on it. She was certain that it would be her that would die.

However, when the overdose failed her thoughts went from suicide to homicide rather quickly. But the intended victim had not been her mother.

Her plan had been to get a hold of Carlos the next day and kill him. She figured she could catch him after first hour and slash his throat if she snuck up behind him. She believed that if she couldn't have him then no one should be allowed to have him. He belonged to her essentially.

However, the one obstacle in her plan to kill Carlos was the meeting they had with the guidance counselor the next day. Nikki was unsure whether she would be sent home after the meeting or not. In order to kill Carlos she would have to skip the guidance meeting. So, in order to accomplish this, she figured she would have to kill her parents as well. She would just wait until they were sleeping and then simply slash their throats. Then they could no longer stand in her way.

A real obstacle came into this metaphorical plan when her father left for church after dinner that night alone and her mother stayed home. This was very out of character for them. Nikki also stayed home as her mother told her she was grounded for the rest of the evening. She was instructed to clean the dishes after dinner.

Nikki decided that she would just roll with this change. She believed, since she was now home alone with her mother, that it would be much easier to kill her mother now, clean up the mess, and then wait until her father returned. She could then kill him and do the same. Finally, she could drive herself to school in the morning, wait for Carlos, and kill him after first hour just like she had planned. It would work out perfectly.

Logical thought was gone at this point in time. Nikki was acting strictly on whatever thoughts came to her mind and they were frantic, desperate. Still, she waited for her opportunity to arrive. She waited for her moment when she could kill her mother.

Opportunity came while she was cleaning up in the kitchen and Billie Jean was working at her computer. Nikki took a kitchen knife, paused for a moment to check the blade for its sharpness, and then slowly approached her mother. She hesitated now that she had the knife in hand. She wasn't sure what it would feel like to slash someone's throat.

When she finally got up the nerve to come up behind her mother and attempt to cut her throat it didn't slash it, it only cut it. Billie Jean jumped up in surprise and darted towards the laundry room. She screamed, "No, Nikki, no."

"I told her I had to kill her because I can't live without Carlos," Nikki explained to police in her interview.

Nikki kept stabbing her because she wanted to put her out of her misery, she claims. She didn't want her mother to suffering any longer. And in her last moments, Billie Jean still offered her daughter forgiveness for killing her.

Nikki spent one night in the hospital because of her claim of ingesting a large amount of Aspirin. After that she was turned over to the county jail where she was formally booked on a charge of First Degree Murder.

The First Trial

The first trial for Nikki Reynolds lasted from April 14, 1999 – May 3, 1999.

If convicted, Nikki faced life in prison after spending two years in a Juvenile Detention Centre. The prosecution built their case around Nikki's obsession with Carlos Infante, making sure to indicate that he was not at fault in any way and rather he was also one of the three listed on Nikki's kill list.

The defence opted to take an insanity plea route, rather than try to dispute the charge that Nikki had committed the murder – something she had confessed to multiple times. This defence fell flat. The criterion for an insanity plea is very strict. The accused has to suffer from a serious mental illness and the accused has to be unaware that what they are doing is wrong or has consequences.

The psychologist that testified for the prosecution indicated that Nikki was well aware of what she was doing, and rather that she was just a confused girl. The defence tried to argue that Nikki suffered from Borderline Personality disorder. They claimed that individuals suffering from this disorder could idolize the individuals they are with and then suddenly snap, and become violent. Which is very similar to Nikki's reaction after Carlos indicated he wanted nothing to do with her. They also claimed that the Aspirin played a part as Aspirin can cause metabolic imbalances and psychosis upon overdoes.

Regardless of the claims on either side, the jury was hung and the trial ended in a mistrial.

The Second Trial

Second trail for Nikki Reynolds began on Sept 1, 1999.

Similar to the first, the prosecution brought a series of psychologists to the stand to prove that, while not a rational act, Nikki was not insane. The prosecution also claimed that her mother's death was premeditated.

The defence countered that Nikki was mentally ill and called experts to speak to Nikki's sanity. The defence also brought forward Nikki's biological mother to testify. The birth mother had a long history of mental illness and family violence. The defence argued that it was the anxiety over losing Carlos that pushed Nikki over the edge and brought her mental illness to the surface.

After much deliberation, Nikki Reynolds was found guilty of Second Degree Murder at the end of the trial.

At the sentencing hearing on January 7, 2000 Nikki's biological mother made a plea to include treatment as a part of Nikki's sentence. She believed that her daughter needed help, much like she had needed help in her lifetime.

Nikki also addressed the court, pleading with the judge to sentence her to a psychiatric facility instead of prison. She truly believed that there had been something wrong that day, if not insanity, than something else. She believed that she needed help. She bore no ill will towards her family. She hated none of them. She had never hated them and still didn't.

However, the judge believed that the wrongness of what she had done to outweigh all else. He gave her the maximum sentence under Florida law, 34 years in prison. She was resentenced to 21 years and 8 months on April 4, 2001 due to a change in sentencing laws in the state of Florida.

In the end Robert Reynolds remarried in 1998 and has had no contact with his daughter since she was sent to prison on January 2000.

And Nikki was incarcerated at the Gadsden Correctional Facility in Quincy, Florida. She was eligible for parole in 2015 and was released.

PSYCHO GIRL : THE TRUE STORY OF CATHERINE BIRNIE

76

JENA DICKENS

Catherine Margaret Harrison was born on May 23rd, 1951. Her partner, David John Birnie, was born on February 16th, 1951 and died on October 7th, 2015 by way of suicide. The duo was famously known throughout Australia as: The Killer Couple. They were from Perth, Australia and were found to have murdered four women ranging in age from 15 to 31 years old, over a span of about five weeks. Their fifth victim managed to escape through the bedroom window, while Catherine was distracted by a knock at the front door. The woman immediately ran and found help. The press referred to the heinous murders as the Moorhouse Murders. The victims were taken to Catherine and David's home located at 3 Moorhouse Street in Willagee, in Western Australia, a suburb of Perth.

Catherine was only two years old when her mother died in childbirth while giving birth to Catherine's younger brother. Her brother also died, two days later. Catherine's father, Harold, couldn't manage raising Catherine on his own at that time so she went to live with her maternal grandparents. When she was ten years old, Harold petitioned the court to receive custody of Catherine again, and he won. There always seemed to be a battle. Catherine's father didn't want her, but then wanted her, always back and forth. After Catherine was convicted of four counts of murder, it caused her father to suffer a nervous breakdown.

When Catherine was twelve years old she met a boy named David Birnie and they began dating two years later when they became teenagers. Both Catherine and David came from dysfunctional families. Their home life was chaotic and messy, literally as well as figuratively. David's mother was an alcoholic and his father was away at work the majority of the time. His father died in 1986 after battling a long illness. The house, as well as his mother, were messy and unkempt. She left her older children in charge of taking care of their younger siblings. She refused to do anything when it concerned the children and their welfare. Allegedly, David's mother would leave the refrigerator door open so that the children could eat throughout the day. David was the oldest of five children. David's school friends, as well as the local priest, deemed the family dysfunctional. The parents never prepared meals for their children, the house was always a mess, and the Priest, before marrying David's parents, said that he felt that their marriage would never lead to anything good. Little did he know how accurate his assumptions would be.

Catherine and David met through mutual friends shortly after David's family moved to the same Perth neighborhood as Catherine and her father. Catherine's father felt that David was trouble and a bad influence. Catherine had begun getting into a lot of trouble with the local police ever since the two of them met. Harold begged and pleaded with Catherine to stay away from David and stay out of trouble. Of course, this just brought the two closer. Whenever two kids are told not to do something, they go out of their way to blatantly disobey.

Even in adolescence David began exhibiting violent and perverse behavior. When David turned fifteen he dropped out of school and began working as jockey apprentice for Eric Parnham at the Ascot Race Course. While there, David would hurt the horses and also began his perverse career as an exhibitionist. David committed his first rape shortly after. By this point he had spent time in and out of jail for several charges ranging from misdemeanors to felonies. He built up a reputation around town as a sex and pornography addict.

Catherine was an accessory to a lot of crimes because of her involvement with David. They built up an extensive history of numerous charges including: breaking and entering, trespassing, unlawfully driving a motor vehicle, and theft. Catherine took the time, while in jail, to decide it was time to get away from David and start over. David had to serve a long jail sentence, while Catherine got off with probation. With the help of her parole officer, she found a job as a housekeeper working for the McLaughlin family. She ended up marrying the families' oldest son, Donald McLaughlin, on her twenty first birthday. They went on to have seven children. One of her children, however, was killed in a car accident while he was only an infant, leaving her with six of her children to take care of. Catherine was never really interested in motherhood though, and wasn't proud of her children and her family like another mother might be. She wasn't concerned about the children or keeping up with the house. Catherine was never truly happy. Her thoughts kept going back to her childhood love, David Birnie. The family that she had left never saw Catherine as a violent or evil person. Not unless she was around David.

Catherine finally reconnected with David Birnie after a thirteen year separation, four weeks after she gave birth to their seventh child. David had escaped from prison and the two of them had begun seeing each other. Catherine left her family and everything behind when David popped back into her life. They finally moved in together and Catherine had her last name changed to Birnie, although the couple never formally or legally got married. They moved into a white brick, two bedroom bungalow on Moorhouse Street. The house was unkempt, the property looked untended, and the house needed a fresh coat of paint. Catherine was completely dependent on David, emotionally and physically. Catherine was easily controlled and manipulated by David, and she would do anything and everything to make him happy. She never wanted to disappoint him. David had an insatiable sexual appetite and was said to have sex up to six times a day. He also accrued an extensive pornography collection and his brother claimed he always had someone. He always had a woman around. David's brother, James, had ended up staying with Catherine and David for a short while. James had just recently been released from prison after serving time for his own sex related offenses. He stayed with the couple for about six months. His brother went on to describe the numbing spray that David would spray on his penis before he had sex with all of the different women.

David and Catherine had exhausted all of their options sexually and began looking for new ways to pleasure themselves. They had spoken about abduction and rape, but had not realized that it would be just a few short weeks before they turned their fantasies into a heinous and perverted reality. Being as emotionally dependent on David as she was, it was easy for David to talk her into his abduction and rape plans. Catherine could never tell him no. She felt that she couldn't survive without him and would do anything to keep him. Catherine was completely codependent and David always seemed to be in control. She wanted David to have all the pleasure and excitement that he wanted but knew that they had exhausted all efforts between just the two of them.

The abductions, rapes, and brutal murders began on October 6th, 1986. The couple didn't really care who their victims were, as long as they were female and alone. Twenty two year old Mary Neilson arrived at the Moorhouse Street residence to inquire about some tires that David had for sale. Mary was a student at the University of Western Australia where she was pursuing her degree in Psychology. Once inside the house, David took Mary by knife point and chained her to their bed and gagged her. Catherine stood in the room and watched as David raped the girl repeatedly. After the rape, the couple took Mary to Gleneagles National Park. David raped her one more time and then strangled her with a nylon cord and stabbed her through the heart. The couple then buried Mary in a shallow grave. Catherine looked on while David committed these violent acts, however, she did not yet participate.

The second murder took place on October 20th. The victim was fifteen year old, Susannah Candy. Susannah was a high school student attending Hollywood High School. She lived with her parents and had two brothers and one sister. Catherine and David Birnie had been driving around for several hours that night in search of their next victim. The couple finally found a girl walking along Stirling Highway, by herself, trying to hitch a ride. As soon as she got into David's car she had a knife to her throat and she was taken to the Birnies' home. While at the home, she was forced to write letters to her family explaining that she decided to run away. David repeatedly raped Susannah while she lay bound and gagged. Catherine had gotten into the bed with them and tried to strangle her with the nylon cord, but Susannah began fighting back. They forced sleeping pills down her throat, and once she passed out they successfully strangled her with the cord. The couple took Susannah to the State Park and buried her in a shallow grave, like their previous victims. This was the first time that Catherine took part in the murder. Catherine never showed any form of remorse over what she had done. When later asked why she contributed she said, "I wanted to see how strong I was within my inner self. I didn't feel a thing. It was like I expected. I was prepared to follow him to the end of the earth and do anything to see that his desires were satisfied. She was a female. Females hurt and destroy males."

On November 1st, the Killer Couple comes across their third victim, Noelene Patterson. Noelene was on her way home from work when her car ran out of gas. Noelene was a bar manager and had been working at Nedland's Golf Club that day. She was standing beside her car when David pulled up to her and offered his help. The thirty one year old got into David's car and was immediately met with a knife at her throat. She was taken to Moorhouse Street where she was bound and gagged, while being raped repeatedly. The original plan, like the others, was to kill the girl that same night. David had seemed to develop feelings for Noelene however. Catherine noticed the fondness that David had for the woman and became extremely jealous and increasingly upset. Noelene represented the type of person that Catherine could only wish to be and she absolutely despised her because of this. Catherine gave David an ultimatum at this point. She put the knife to her own chest and said, 'you either kill her tonight, or I will kill myself.' It was on the third night, after being given the ultimatum, that David gave Noelene several sleeping pills and then strangled her. She was then taken to the park and buried beside the other victims. Catherine admitted to taking pleasure in throwing sand in the victims face as David coldly buried her with no remorse.

Catherine and David's fourth victim, Denise Brown, suffered the same fate as the previous women who had the unfortunate experience of crossing paths with the Killer Couple. Denise Brown was twenty one years old, and was taken on November 5, 1986 while waiting at a bus stop. She was gagged and raped repeatedly before being put into the car and taken to Pine Plantation, where she was raped again while David waited for a blanket of darkness to fall. After it got dark he took her out and raped her again, while stabbing her in the neck. As David began burying her, thinking she was dead, Denise surprised the couple by sitting straight up in her grave. David struck her in the head twice with an axe as Catherine looked on in shock and amazement. David has said that he learned bodies would decompose at a faster rate if you stabbed them.

Detective Sergeant Paul Ferguson was the first to realize that he could be dealing with a serial killer, after the fourth woman was reported missing. Years later he recalled his experience while working on the case. He recalls how this case still haunts him and when asked why replied, "Because it was the most interesting and horrific I've had in my career," and "I have things tucked away back here that I pray to God I never pull out of the drawer." All of the missing women had come from relatively good homes and they never got into any real trouble. Their families found the phone calls and letters they received very suspicious.

The couples' fifth and final victim was seventeen year old Kate Moir. She was on her way home, after a night out with her friends, when she was abducted by the couple. The date of this final abduction was November 10th, 1986. Kate was the only one of their victims that was able to escape and run and find help. David had left the house for work that day. Catherine was home with Kate. She forced her to call her parents and tell them that she would be staying at a friend's house. When Catherine heard a knock at the door, she left Kate alone, untied, and went to see who was there. Kate took the opportunity to escape through the open window and ran half naked to the nearest store. She ran in crying and pleading for help. Kate was taken to the Palmyra police station and questioned. She was able to give the police a full description of Catherine and David, as well as inform the police of the couples' address. After their arrest, Catherine admitted to knowing Kate, but the couple said that the sexual acts were consensual and she was a willing participant. The police performed a search of the Birnie's home and found Kate's bag, as well as a pack of cigarettes that Kate had managed to hide in the ceiling in order to prove that she was there. After hours of questioning, Catherine and David finally admitted to the rape and murders of the four women and agreed to show the police where they had buried them. Three of the victims had been buried in Gleneagle State Forest and one on the Pine Plantation. The couple showed no emotion, whatsoever, as the police dug up the graves. David was the one who showed the police the locations of the women, except for one. Catherine insisted that she be the one to show them where Noelene was buried. She showed no regret, only anger. She spat on Noelene's grave and made her strong feelings of hate toward her very vocal to the detective. She explained to the police, in great detail, how much she despised Noelene Patterson. As they were leaving, David turned to Detective Katich and said chillingly, "What a pointless loss of young life." They showed absolutely no remorse for what they had done. This statement stuck with the detectives for years to follow. They couldn't believe how little the couple seemed to care or regret what they had been done. In some ways, however, they thought Catherine was relieved that it was finally over.

Catherine admitted to not caring about participating in the rapes and murders of the women, until they got to Denise Brown. "I think I must have come to a decision that sooner or later there had to be an end to the rampage. I had reached the stage when I didn't know what to do. I suppose I came to a decision that I was prepared to give her a chance." The brutal manner in which Denise was murdered seemed to hit Catherine hard. She witnessed David not only stab her repeatedly but strike her in the head with the axe. "Deep and dark in the back of my mind was yet another fear. I had a great fear that I would have to look at another killing like that of Denise Brown, the girl he murdered with the axe."

In response to Kate Moir's escape, due to Catherine's carelessness with her victim, she said, "I knew that it was a foregone conclusion that David would kill her, and probably do it that night. I was just fed up with the killings.

I thought if something did not happen soon it would simply go on and on and never end."

Kate Moir survived the abduction and attacks of Australia's most infamous serial killers. Instead of remaining a victim, she chose to be a survivor. She also sought to seek reform for the way her government handled cases like hers.

"I want to see no parole for wilful murder. I want a reintroduction of wilful murder as a charge. I want truth in sentencing. I want no parole for sex offenders and child sex offenders. We have been softening our justice system for years."

Kate Moir is a married woman and mother of three children. She constantly fights for the changes and justice she deserves. The following are quotes that were made by Kate, again concerning Catherine's parole and the possibility of her release.

"I want the legacy that I leave to be that of a survivor and a hero, not a victim. But enough is enough."

"I want the Attorney General to change the law and stop reviewing Catherine Birnie's parole. She does not apply for it herself, it is automatically reviewed and every time it happens, it causes me incredible pain."

"Every time I hear that her parole is being reviewed, I relive the nightmare. It causes significant trauma because I relive it and it feels like it happened yesterday. My name was always protected because I was a minor at the time I was captured, but due to the internet, if anybody googles my name it is everywhere and linked to the Birnie killings."

The couple appeared in court on November 12th, 1986. This was just two days after their fifth victim had escaped and they were arrested. The court proceedings took place at Fremantle Magistrates Court. They both refused any kind of representation, no plea was entered, bail was refused, and they were remanded into custody. Catherine allegedly took photos and the couple also recorded video of their criminal acts. At trial, the police were in possession of the video evidence. On February 10, 1987 a crowd gathered outside of the courthouse. When they saw the couple being ushered in for trial they screamed and chanted, "Hang the Bastards!" The community was outraged over the news of the serial killings that took place and wanted David and Catherine to receive the maximum sentence. They even wanted to reinstate the death penalty for David and Catherine Birnie.

Bill Power, the court reporter, spoke about the proceedings and the manners in which the couple acted while in court. He said that it would be something that would always stick with him, he would never forget.

"*There was nothing distinctive about David and Catherine when they first appeared in court to face multiple murder charges in the serial killings which brought an end to the mystery of young women going missing off Perth streets.*"

"*They were a rather nondescript, ordinary looking couple you might find running a petrol station in a country town. David was a weedy little man and Catherine his drab, slightly buxom wife with a very sour face. Both were accompanied by male police officers.*"

"*If you have ever witnessed a wild cat go off, then try and imagine some hellcat in the confined spaces of a narrow staircase. Catherine Birnie fought against the guarding police officers and refused to allow any of them to touch her as she screamed and spat her words at them until she reached the dock and spotted her beloved, David. Only then did she calm down.*"

It had also been said previously, by some people in the community that the couple never looked like the type that could commit such violent acts. They looked like normal and ordinary people. But the secret horrors of what occurred in their home on Moorhouse Street would paint a very different image of the couple.

Trial Judge Justice Wallace said in trial, "Each of these horrible crimes were premeditated, planned, and carried out cruelly and relentlessly over a comparatively short period."

Right before Judge Wallace sentenced Catherine, he delivered the following message to her. He explained that he did not believe that even though she pled guilty, that she was truly sorry for what she had done. She had pled guilty and avoided a long trial, and spared the victims' families from having to relive over and over what happened to their loved ones, but she showed no remorse, no emotion, no sympathy for the crimes she had committed with David Birnie.

"You willingly joined in the selection of your unfortunate victims, carried them off at knifepoint, and held them in captivity for the sole purpose of the sexual gratification of your partner in crime and then murdered them, lest you be identified, and then finally mutilated them. You personally extinguished the life of two of your victims and certainly participated in the death of the third. The only appropriate punishment is the sentence I intend to impose, strict life security in prison."

Remember, Catherine was completely devoted, obsessed, and brainwashed when it came to David. She would do anything and everything for him to make sure he was happy. This is the driving factor that David used to manipulate and control her. He needed an accomplice and she was more than willing, and he knew it. Catherine and David received four separate life sentences for the abduction, torture, rape, and murder of Mary Neilson, Susannah Candy, Noelene Patterson, and Denise Brown. Under sentencing laws, their case was brought up every three years automatically for parole. Kate began a crusade to ensure that the couple remained in prison. She grew a social media presence and page entitled, We Support Kate, as well as worked with the Empowerment Foundation in an attempt to build an online reform petition. Kate also received support from Catherine's son, Peter. He chose not to release his surname to the public, due to the physical and emotional abuse he has been forced to face in relation to his mother's crimes. He had suffered personal and professional ruin, as soon as people learned about his family history. He had been turned down for jobs, lost jobs he had, and even lost his fiancé because of his family background. Peter was only five years old when his mother was arrested. He saw his mother on television because of it shortly after her arrest. When speaking out on the abuse he faced, he recalled horrible stories of what happened to him, and his siblings, while growing up. He also stated that the mandatory parole hearings, every three years, prevented him from getting on with his life. Having to hear about his mother and relive the violence his mother was responsible for every few years, was an interruption to his life, and it made it harder to maintain a sense of normalcy within his career life and personal life. In an interview with the West Australian, Peter stated, "I want the parole board to hear I don't want her out. I don't want to see her out." He also said, "I have had baseball bats to the head, I have been jumped on and kicked at. I have been knocked out."

After pleading guilty and receiving their sentences, David was initially sent to maximum security Fremantle Prison, he was eventually moved into solitary confinement. He did not get along with the other prisoners and was constantly getting into fights. The inmates frequently and violently attacked David. A day before he was due in trial for the charge of rape of an inmate, David hung himself in his jail cell. His suicide occurred in 2009 at Casuarina Prison. Catherine's request to attend David's funeral was refused.

Catherine was sent to Bandyup Women's prison where she was eventually employed as the head librarian. While in prison, the couple exchanged over 2600 letters, but were denied any other form of contact. Catherine's mandatory parole hearings were finally revoked in 2009, and her papers were subsequently marked: 'never to be released.'

While many people are against Catherine Birnie ever getting parole, one man stands against this argument. Perth QC Tom Percy disagrees with the opinion of people that had been saying that some people just don't deserve a second chance. The following quotes by Percy outline his argument of Catherine not remaining in prison and the likelihood of her harming the community, as well as his stance of being in favor of Catherine's parole.

"She should not be kept in prison to satisfy society's thirst for revenge."

"She has been there thirty odd years and you would think it might be time for us to say she has done her time. She has done her statutory minimum prescribed by the court, which was in possession of all of the facts."

"I am not sure she could really be a threat to anyone anymore, and all my information from Bandyup Womens' Prison is that she is a little old granny that goes about her work in the library like a church mouse."

"This case just so happened to be one that caught the public attention, even though she was not the prime mover in it. David is now dead."

"What's the point of keeping her in there? Sadly, it looks like she will never get parole, but I think she probably deserves it."

Despite his argument and fight to get Catherine released from prison, she still remains behind bars. She has not requested any new parole hearings, herself, as of yet. Some people in the community had gone as far as to say that if she were to be released, then maybe Percy should allow her to live with him in his residence.

It was now January of 1987. A letter written by Catherine Birnie, while in prison, eventually surfaced. It was a letter she had written to her six children in an attempt to explain some of her actions that led to her being placed in prison and why she left them in the first place. The letter reads as followed:

"Dear kids, Hi! Mum here...the reason I changed my name to Birnie was so that you kids wouldn't be hurt by the newspapers and television people. I am not proud of what has been said about me, but I have to live with that and the memories. As to why this happened, I can only hope that the doctors can help me to find out.....I never stopped loving any of you kids. Maybe I was wrong about leaving you but I thought you would be safer with your father."

Catherine's husband, Donald, claimed that he had still wanted her back. This was after trial and after he heard of the horrific acts she had committed with David. He stated, 'you can't stop loving someone after fifteen years of marriage.' Donald's mother stood firmly beside her son, saying that Catherine had been good and non-violent, until David cast his spell over her. Catherine's nephew, Leonard Nock, stood beside his aunt claiming, "All Aunt Cathy wanted was someone to lean on. She never had a mother. She is a very caring person. She and I are very close. I used to call her my mum. She was never the violent type, she never used to hit the kids. It is not the Cathy we used to know and love." In Catherine's letter she also persuaded the children to tell their father to divorce her. She said their father needed to move on and this was the way it needed to be done. She didn't hold out any hope for her eventual release and didn't want Donald to wait for her, because it was never going to happen. She also asked the children to get permission from Donald to write back to her, and maybe even one day go and visit her. The family put the entirety of the blame on David. They refused to admit to or believe that Catherine had anything to do with the violence. During their prison visits, the family also failed to even ask Catherine the question regarding her guilt or innocence. They didn't want to hear the answer, therefore, they never even asked the question.

Catherine Bernie was up for parole in 2013 and again in 2016. She was denied both years. She is once again up for review sometime in 2019. "Now barring any reason to keep her in, and revenge I don't consider enough of a reason. She should be released."-Percy

Despite Percy's statements, Catherine Birnie remains in prison to this very day, with little to no chance of parole. People, even to this day, wonder if the abductions, the perverse rape, and heinous murders would have continued long past the few weeks they had gotten away with it. If they had never been caught, would they have continued? Finally, were there other victims that they never confessed to? Other gravesites that have yet to be located? It is too late for David Birnie to tell anyone, but Catherine still has the chance to admit to any other wrongdoing she had done before her permanent home in prison forced her to keep distance between herself and her lover. I guess we will never know.

"I honestly believe that woman has never given those victims one ounce of consideration, both the dead victims and the families of the victims...They [David and Catherine Birnie] were parasites who lived off of each other. The most evil people I have ever, ever come across."-Detective Paul Ferguson.

BABY KILLER

The True Story of Amelia Dyer

Chrissy Eubank

Amelia Dyer, considered one of the most prolific serial killers in history, was born around 1837 in Victorian Britain. Her picture on the front cover easily betrays the evil that resided within her heart. Her reign of terror lasted over twenty years, as she is projected to have killed as many as 400 children before finally being caught

She embarked on a thirty year career of killing with eyewitnesses seeing at least six babies entering her house a day. The count of 400 dead is a conservative estimate.

EARLY LIFE

Amelia was the youngest of five children born into the tiny town of Pyle Marsh. She had three older brothers, Thomas, James, and William along with an older sister named Ann. Her father was a shoemaker named Samuel Hobley and her mother was named Sarah Weymouth.

But he didn't come from an impoverished family like so many others during the Victorian Era.

"For the time, she had a pretty good start," said author Allison Rattle. "Her father had a pretty good trade and paid for her to go to church and school which at the time only a quarter of the children her age actually got an education so she was privileged in that respect."

She found entertainment in reading and used to write poetry herself. Amelia's mother Sarah, however, became mentally ill after suffering from typhus fever. Amelia had to suffer through watching her mother's seizures and outbursts, providing care for her until she died in 1848.

"She witnessed her mother basically losing her mind," said Rattle. "And dying a slow, horrific death. I guess being a young girl she may have been called upon to nurse her mother slightly or at least wait upon her."

Psychologists have posited that it was going through this trauma of watching her mother lose her mind, that caused Amelia's own emotional wiring to run askew.

"Amelia would later claim that her mother died as a result of hereditary insanity," said author Allison Vale. "I think though that this isn't true but it's really easy to understand how she could have remembered it that way."

"It was certain to have a massive impact on her and she may have learned a few things about what kind of symptoms might be shown by someone whose losing their mind."

Amelia was sent to live with her aunt in nearby Bristol after her mother's death. She started an apprenticeship with a corset maker and worked there until her father died in 1859. The oldest brother, Thomas, took control of the family shoe business. Two years later, some type of estrangement occurred with her brothers, specifically James and Amelia doesn't appear to have further ties with her family.

In 1861, Amelia moved to Trinity Street, Bristol. She married George Thomas, who at 59 years old was 35 years Amelia's senior. The two lied about their ages on their marriage certificate with George claiming he was 48 years old and Amelia claiming she was 30.

A CAREER IN "HEALTH CARE"

Amelia began training as a nurse after she got married.

"Amelia turned to one of the most arduous professions she could have turned to," Vale said. "Nursing was just starting to change. It was post-Crimean war. Nursing was starting to have a much better profile as a result of Florence Nightingale. But it was still a thankless profession."

"It wasn't a caring profession like it is present day," agreed psychologist Laura Richards. "They train you psychologically to be a lot more robust around dealing with people. So she became quite hardy and emotionless from having been trained through the nursing regime."

Amelia became pregnant at the age of twenty-six before she met a woman named Ellen Dane who came to boarder at her house. Dane was a midwife who told her of a lucrative and shady way to earn money. Amelia would use her own home as a front to provide housing for women who had gotten pregnant out of wedlock. They would them give the babies away for adoption or kill them through malnutrition.

They called it baby farming.

"Amelia could see it was a very easy way to make money," Rattle said. "Although with risks involved obviously although Amelia did have training as a mid-wife as well through her nursing experience so it was certainly something she knew she was capable of doing. That was the beginning of a massive change in Amelia's life."

Dane moved her base of operations to the USA while Amelia took her "business plan" to heart. During this time, unmarried mothers did not have access to any kind of subsidy as the 1834 Poor Law Amendment Act did not oblige the fathers of illegitimate children to pay for their upbringing. These laws, coupled with the stigmatization of single mothers, forced the practice of baby farming.

Amelia discussed business strategies with Dane. She knew the best bet was to insist on being paid upfront with a one-time fee. She refused any type of money for continuous care as she knew that would mean the mother would return to visit.

"The one off premiums were certainly not enough to sustain a child's life for long financially," Vale said. "And the only way that it would be profitable for a baby farmer was to subject a child to persist underfeeding that would at some point bring about the infant's death."

"Abortion was not an option," Judith Knelman said. "So the simplest thing to do was hide, have the baby and get rid of it. Pay somebody to take care of it or pay somebody to get rid of it."

The babies were subsequently left on the premises and seen as "nurse children."

"Illegitimacy was seen as hugely immoral," said author Allison Rattle. "Even orphanages would only accept orphans from families where the parents were married and the father had died. They wouldn't accept a child who was born out of wedlock."

"Dickens did a really good job of describing social conditions in the 1850 and 60s," Knelman added. "Certainly there were a lot of poor people. There were a lot of neglected and abandoned children."

"There was no work," said Alan McCormick of Scotland Yard. "There was no social services. There was no welfare. One in every twelve women was a prostitute. A child being born in normal circumstances only had a fifty percent chance of reaching the age of five. So that's how bad it was."

BABY FARMING

"Baby farming was a business carried out throughout the country," said historian Ken Wells. "If a mother was unable to look after their child, there was an option of sending them out to a baby farmer, also known as fostering, with the understanding that they could visit the child whenever they wanted to."

On the surface they were providing a service to a growing need. They took an unwanted child and gave them to a foster parent. Only those foster parents and caregivers didn't always have the best interests of the infant at heart.

"MOTHER'S FRIEND"

The majority of these "caregivers" resorted to starving out the babies. They sedated crying babies with alcohol or drugs usually using Godfrey's Cordial, also known as 'Mother's Friend'. This syrup was one of the most popular medicines given to infants and children in both the United States and England in the latter years of the 18th and early 19th centuries. The syrup was used as a panacea to everything from colic to jaundice to excessive crying to diarrhea. 'Mother's Friend' was harmful despite its harmless sounding name as it contained one grain of opium for every two ounces. Many infants were poisoned from this syrup which was administered in secret by nurses who wanted to keep babies under their care in a deep state of sleep and thus more manageable.

"A hungry child, a noisy child, is a difficult child to raise," author Allison Vale said. "And something that was chillingly referred to colloquially as 'the Quietness' was an over the counter anti-colic cordial and it did contain liquid opium which was laudanum and in some cases brandy."

"People gave babies laudanum when they were supposed to be giving them food," Klansman said. "Because it dulled the need, or dulled the awareness of the baby that it was hungry. Of course it didn't nourish the baby so eventually a baby that was given that and not given enough food would die."

The babies would die from severe malnutrition but the coroner would record the death as "debility from birth", "lack of breast milk" or "starvation."

There were those guilt-ridden mothers who returned to the baby-farming homes to check on their children but would find their efforts blocked. Most would be too scared or embarrassed to inform the police of any wrongdoing. The police themselves had numerous problems tracking any children that were deemed missing.

"Dead infants," Vale said. "Or abandoned infants were as commonplace in British cities as roadkill today. Babies were found parceled up in railroad stations, under railroad arches."

"It was desperation," McCormick added. "For the vast majority of these ladies."

TO A MANNER BORN

With Dane's departure to the States, Amelia set her sights on taking her place in the baby-farming business. She had just given birth to her own daughter, Ellen, but in 1869 her husband George died.

A widow at age 32 with a baby, Amelia needed a new source of income...

She began taking in pregnant women as she placed ads to nurse and adopt the babies. In return, she required a large one-time fee and clothing for the child. She began meeting with expectant young women, convincing them that she was someone who could be trusted in providing a safe and loving home for their child.

Before she followed through with her plan, however, she put her own child up for adoption and sent her away.

"It was a choice that she made," Vale said. "She had options. She could have worked through. But instead what she does is to farm her own child out and opt for the easy money that she seemed to be able to make."

"As Amelia chose to go into the baby farming business," Rattle said. "She was maybe able to travel around here, there and everywhere adopting babies so it made sense for her daughter to be out of the way."

Three years after her first husband George died, Amelia remarried. His name was William Dyer, a brewers laborer from Bristol. They had two children together, Mary Ann aka Polly and William Samuel.

Amelia eventually left William, however, as the latter lost his job and offered little in the way of finances.

Strapped for cash, Amelia decided to dispense with the heavy cost of letting the babies die through neglect and starvation. So after each child was born she promptly murdered them, thus incurring a windfall of profits.

"Baby farmers used different methods," Klansman said. "Some of which are less palatable than others."

"Quite often she would suffocate babies at birth," Rattle said. "Smothering the baby the moment its head came out, before it turned blue as that would be a sign that it had taken its first breath. (She made) it would look like a stillbirth so the death certificate would all be above board."

When her daughter Polly asked why so many babies came and disappeared, Amelia described herself as the "angel maker."

"I'm sending little children to Jesus," Amelia said. "Because he wanted them far more than their mothers did."

"Cold," Alan McCormick of New Scotland Yard said in describing Amelia. "Those kids meant nothing to her. It was just a means of getting money."

It can be argued, however, that once Amelia got a taste of killing she did it more for the power than the money and greed.

"The actual killing of the child," Holmes said. "Watching the child peacefully to some degree die. It parallels perhaps seeing her mother pass away where she felt an almost God-like power over these children that she had decided were going to go to their maker."

AROUSING SUSPICION

"Amelia was already aware of the fact that this was not going to be about her helping children," forensic psychologist David Holmes said. "This was going to be a fairly cruel and anti-mothering act that would be carried out in order to gain all of this money."

Amelia successfully avoided police involvement until 1879, a good ten years into her murderous ways. A doctor became suspicious about the number of child deaths he had been called in to certify under Amelia's care.

"The inquests were held in Somerset," Vale said. "And they're (the police) pretty certain that the babies have died as a direct result of neglect and opium overdose. But they can't prove it. And interestingly, she gets off with a six months sentence with hard labor."

Without a coroner that was able to rule completely against her, Amelia would have undoubtedly been executed by hanging.

"Its incredibly really," Rattle said. "That she only got six months. And there was one example, we read of a chap who got twelve months for stealing a piece of bacon."

Amelia took the punishment hard, becoming an emotional wreck during her jail stay. She resumed her business, however, as soon as she was released.

"In the long term," Holmes reasoned. "It mostly would have served as a very hard lesson in forensic awareness that she wasn't gonna get caught again. And there was no way she was going to leave any evidence which had been the problem in leading up to her capture."

She was sent to mental hospitals for supposed mental illness and suicidal ideations but these seemed to be well-timed acts. From her experience of working in an asylum, Amelia knew the tricks of the trade in order to make her stay an easy one.

"I don't think Amelia Dyer was insane," said Vale. "I think she was a very bad person who deliberately committed murder for profit."

Amelia had both an alcohol and substance abuse problem, using on a regular basis as she began her killings once again.

"Certainly the drugs would have had an impact on her," Richards said. "On her mental state. Maybe induced this complete detachment from reality."

"A long term laudanum habit," Vale concurred. "Will lead to periods of depression. It can lead to mood swings even when you're not under the influence. I think it also exacerbates any underlying mental health issues."

RETURNING TO BABY FARMING

In 1884, British society took a much harder line against baby farming and any sign of neglect or abuse would be reported.

"She definitely changes her modus operandi at this point (after 1884)," Vale said. "She's beginning to murder these children."

In 1890, Amelia took on the care of the illegitimate baby of a governess. She had begun targeting the babies of the more affluent because of the larger amounts of money involved. The higher up the social class the woman was, however, the more risk was involved as the woman may have means to question and come after Amelia.

"This was a young governess who fell in love with the young master of the house that she worked in and had got pregnant," Rattle said. "She was left on her own and she responds to an advert, gets in touch with Amelia Dyer and moves in with her. Amelia was able to gain the trust of this woman as with many others, so much so that the governess was persuaded to leave her baby in the care of Amelia once it was born."

The governess, however, returned to visit her baby months later and immediately became suspicious that the child she was given was not hers. She stripped the baby to see if a birth mark was present on one of its hips. It wasn't and the governess immediately informed the authorities.

The police, however, could never pin Amelia down.

"She managed to put them off time and time again by sending them on wild goose chases," Rattle said. "She said she had sent them to a couple that moved here...that moved there."

Amelia continued to move from town to town but still found herself being stalked by the governess who wouldn't give up.

"She did feel hounded," Richards said. "I'm sure that would have had an impact on her. She would have felt that pressure."

Amelia then feigned another nervous breakdown and a doctor was brought in. "The birds are telling me to do it! The birds are telling me to do it!" she would cry out, forcing the doctor to send her to an asylum.

"She was a very clever lady," Holmes said. "With the police getting close to her and she needed to lose herself and what better place to go than somewhere like that (a mental asylum)."

Her mental illness continued on unabated as she drank two bottles of laudanum in an attempted suicide. Her long term use of opium, however, allowed her to build up the tolerance necessary to survive.

"Amelia would be drawn to the idea of self-medicating," Holmes said. "Possibly seeing it as a route, a means to ease the situation, make it even easier for her to put up with what she was doing."

"She took it (opium) on a regular basis," Richards said. "She took it almost daily so she was an addict. So that would induce a form of state from her mentally where she would be detached from reality and I think that was part of her coping mechanism to detach from the reality of what she was doing."

After that close call and subsequent hospital release, Amelia resumed baby farming and murder.

"Her mental breakdowns were very short lived," Richards noted. "She would be out of sorts for a period of time that get it all back together again. To me that would say there isn't a mental illness there."

A CLEVER KILLER

She wised up to doing things on the books and decided to stop getting doctors to issue death certificates. Amelia decided to kill and bury the bodies herself. In order to do this, she would have to be a killer on the run as inevitably the mothers would come back seeking to reclaim their children or check on their welfare. Amelia took her family to different cities to escape suspicion as soon as things got too hot. She would use a series of different aliases and rename her businesses.

"Amelia committed what many serial killers do," Holmes explained. "The mistake of accelerating and being over enthusiastic. Either for reasons that she was enjoying the process or quite simply greed was driving her over the edge."

Baby farming began to gain the attention and compassion of the British ruling class, however. They asked why if they had laws for the prevention of the cruelty of animals then why didn't there laws protecting children. With the arrest and hanging of Margaret Waters (another baby farming killer) and the fleeing Dyer, Amelia's colleagues were going downhill fast and perhaps she thought her time was limited.

By 1893, Amelia had another breakdown but was released from the Wells mental asylum. This would be the last time she would be hospitalized. She moved to

Caversham, Berkshire with a woman named Jane "Granny" Smith who didn't know of Amelia's exploits.

"She befriends an old lady named Jane Smith," Vale said. "She's widowed and resigned to spend her last days in the workhouse. Amelia seduces her with stories of rescuing the unwanted infants. Of nursing them. And it's a very, very seductive image. And Jane Smith buys into it, wholesale."

Her daughter Mary Ann aka Polly and her husband Arthur Palmer came along as well.

The group moved to 45 Kensington Road, Reading Berkshire in that same year. Amelia had the perfect front. She coached Jane Smith to call her "mother" in front of prospective clients while Amelia would call her "Granny."

A ruse to project a mother-daughter image and put the guards down of the pregnant young women.

"Jane Smith didn't get the life she was promised at all," Rattle said. "She was treated as no more than a servant really. She was made to look after the children, to clean the house."

Amelia then puts her adoptions into overdrive. The babies come in and out of the house with such rapidity that old lady Jane Smith doesn't even learn their names.

Eyewitnesses later claimed that there were six infants a day coming to and from the house daily.

THE MURDERS CONTINUE

The advertisement in the "Miscellaneous" column of the Bristol Times & Mirror newspaper was poignant.

In January of 1896 a popular barmaid named Evelina Marmon gave birth to a daughter out of wedlock. She named the baby Doris and she sought immediately to have it adopted. She placed an ad in the "Miscellaneous" section of the Bristol Times & Mirror newspaper.

"Wanted, respectable woman to take young child." Marmon intended to go back to work and hoped to eventually reclaim her child.

Evelina was a God-fearing farmer's daughter who left the farm for city life. She found work as a barmaid in the saloon of the Plough Hotel, an old coaching inn. She was buxom with blonde hair and had a vibrant personality. She had plenty of suitors and became pregnant by one of the male patrons who left her deserted.

Evelina knew she could not bring up the baby on her own.

She would have to find a foster home for little Doris - to have her "adopted out", in the language of the time - go back to work and hope in time to be able to reclaim her child.

Next to her own ad was an advertisement that read _"Married couple with no family would adopt healthy child, nice country home. Terms, £10"._

Marmon answered the ad which was addressed to a "Mrs. Harding", an alias of Amelia. A few days later Amelia wrote back, saying _"I should be glad to have a dear little baby girl, one I could bring up and call my own. We are plain, homely people, in fairly good circumstances. I don't want a child for money's sake, but for company and home comfort... Myself and my husband are dearly fond of children. I have no child of my own. A child with me will have a good home and a mother's love. It is just lovely here, heatlhy and pleasant. There is an orchard opposite our front door."_

Evelina was assured that she could visit whenever she wished.

"Rest assured I will do my duty by that dear child. I will be a mother, as far as lies in my power."

"It is just lovely here, healthy and pleasant. There is an orchard opposite our front door."

Evelina tried to negotiate a weekly fee for the care of Doris but Amelia wanted a substantial one-time fee to be paid upfront. Evelina, seemingly with no other choice, agreed to pay the £10, and a week later "Mrs Harding" arrived in Cheltenham.

Evelina was surprised that Amelia aka "Mrs. Harding" was old (59 years) and heavy set (over 210 lbs). She remained reluctant at first but gave in as the elderly woman immediately showed her Doris some affection, covering her with a shawl.

Evelina gave the old lady a cardboard box of clothes she had prepared – nappies, chemises, petticoats, frocks, nightgowns, and a powder box. She also enclosed the money and received a signed receipt from "Mrs.Harding."

She accompanied her baby daughter and her eventual killer to Cheltenham station then on to Gloucester. Evelina stood there crying through the hot steam on the platform as the 5:20 p.m train took her baby away.

When Evelina returned home, she described herself as "a broken woman."

Days later, she received a letter from "Mrs. Harding" offering her assurance that all was well with her daughter. Evelina wrote back but received no replies afterward.

Amelia told Evelina that she would be going to Reading but lied. She traveled to 76 Mayo Road, Willesden, London where her daughter Mary Ann was staying. Amelia then took some white edging tape and wrapped it around the baby's neck, making a strangling knot. The baby did not die immediately.

"I used to like to watch them with the tape around their neck," Amanda said. "But it was soon all over with them."

"The idea of strangling and using the tape may make it seem almost symbolical or bizarre to ourselves," Holmes said. "But in terms of criminal awareness she was aware of the fact that if she tried to suffocate a baby its not always absolutely certain that the baby is dead."

The mother and daughter team wrapped the baby up with a napkin. They kept the clothes that Evelina gave her and hoped to sell it to a pawnbroker. Amelia used some of the money to pay the rent to her landlady and gave the woman a pair of child's boots as a present for her own little girl.

The following day, April 1st of 1896, a young boy named Harry Simmons was taken to the Mayo Road residence. Amelia had no spare white edging tape available and used the tape from Doris' corpse to strangle the year old boy.

The next day both bodies were rolled into a carpet bag, their corpses stacked one on top of the other. Bricks were added inside for additional weight. Amelia headed back toward Reading, taking the bus to Paddington and then the train. She dragged the carpet bag through the streets until she reached the River Thames. She had a secluded spot at Caversham Lock and she forced the carpet bag through the railing and didn't leave until she heard it splash into the waters below.

She didn't know she had a witness as a man passed, hurrying on his way home calling out "Good night."

A SHOCKING DISCOVERY

Ironically, only days before the dumping of the bodies a package was fished out of the Thames by a bargeman. This package was the work of Amelia as she had not weighed it down adequately. It contained the body of a baby girl named Helena Fry. With only a small police force available in Reading, a Constable Anderson made a significant discovery. He found a label from Temple Meads Station, Bristol and he used microscopic analysis of the wrapping paper. He found a faintly legible name. A "Mrs.Thomas" and an address.

The address of Amelia Dyer.

The police immediately placed Amelia's home under surveillance. They did enough research on Amelia and knew that she would "disappear" if she thought she was under suspicion. So they decided they would be better served if they would use a young woman as a decoy to secure a meeting with Amelia and discuss the prospect of using her "adoptive services."

On April 3rd, while Amelia was waiting on the decoy to arrive, she answered the door to a police raid. The smell of decomposing bodies radiated throughout her home but no human remains were found. The police found other evidence, however, such as the white edging tape, telegrams describing adoption arrangements, pawn tickets for children's clothing, receipts for newspaper ads and letters from distraught mothers asking about the welfare of their child.

The police determined that in the few months Amelia had been in Reading at least twenty children had been placed into her care. She had been preparing to move again, this time to the town of Somerset.

Amelia was arrested on April 4th, three days after the murders of Doris Marmon and Harry Simmons. The Thames River was searched and six more bodies were discovered, including Doris and Harry.

Each child had been strangled with the seamstress white tape and Amelia later told police that "was how you could tell it was one of mine."

Eleven days later, Evelina Marmon had been contacted by police as they found her name in items found in Amelia's home. Distraught, she came to identify her daughter's remains.

THE TRIAL OF A KILLER

An inquest was held a month later. Amelia's daughter Mary Ann and her husband Arthur were not charged as there was no direct evidence that they were her accomplices. Arthur was set free because of a confession handwritten by Amelia. She wrote:

Sir will you kindly grant me the favour of presenting this to the magistrates on Saturday the 18th instant I have made this statement out, for I may not have the opportunity then I must relieve my mind I do know and I feel my days are numbered on this earth but I do feel it is an awful thing drawing innocent people into trouble I do know I shal have to answer before my Maker in Heaven for the awful crimes I have committed but as God Almighty is my judge in Heaven a on Hearth neither my daughter Mary Ann Palmer nor her husband Alfred Ernest Palmer I do most solemnly declare neither of them had any thing at all to do with it, they never knew I contemplated doing such a wicked thing until it was to late I am speaking the truth and nothing but the truth as I hope to be forgiven, I myself and I alone must stand before my Maker in Heaven to give an answer for it all witnes my hand

Amelia Dyer.

— April 16, 1896

On May 22nd, 1896, Amelia appeared in court and pleaded guilty to the murder of Doris Marmon. Her family and friends testified that they had their own suspicions about Amelia and spoke of times that she evaded discovery. A man came forth claiming he had seen and spoken to Amelia as she had disposed of two bodies at Caversham Lock proved key to the prosecution.

Amelia used insanity as a defense, offering her stays in mental asylums as proof of her instability. The prosecution, however, argued that her symptoms were well-rehearsed actions to avoid suspicion as both of her hospital stays coincided with times that Amelia felt her murders would be discovered.

The jury took four and a half minutes to find her guilty. Amelia then spent three weeks in her condemned cell, filling five journals with her confessions. A chaplain visited her the night before her execution and asked if she had anything to confess. She offered him her journals, asking "isn't this enough?"

Amelia was then subpoenaed to appear as a witness in her daughter's own trial for murder which was set for a week after her own execution date. The court ruled, however, that Amelia became "legally dead" after she was sentenced and her testimony would be inadmissible.

On the day of her execution, Amelia discovered that the charges against her daughter had been dropped.

On June 10th, 1896, Amelia Dyer was hanged by James Billington at Newgate Prison. Asked on the scaffold if she had anything to say, she said "I have nothing to say."

URBAN LEGEND?

It remains unknown as to why Amelia's daughter Mary Ann aka Polly was never convicted. Her own daughter provided the majority of the testimony that procured the conviction of her mother but nothing is said about her own involvement.

And the baby murders did not stop after Amelia's death.

Two years after her execution, railroad workers inspecting carriages found a parcel tied up with a string inside a siding on the Plymouth express.

Inside was a three-week old baby girl. The infant was shivering and wet...but alive.

A little research showed that the baby was the child of a widow named Jane Hill. Hill had given the baby to a woman named "Mrs. Stewart" for the one time fee of £12.

"The little one would have a good home and a parent's love and care," Mrs. Stewart had written, her prose eerily echoing that of Amelia Dyer. "Mrs. Stewart" had picked up the baby at Plymouth and dumped her on the next train.

The conjecture was that "Mrs. Stewart" was none other than Polly, Amelia's daughter.